# At Issue

# The Rising Cost of College

# Other Books in the At Issue Series:

# At Issue

# The Rising Cost of College

*Ronald D. Lankford Jr., Book Editor*

**GREENHAVEN PRESS**

*A part of Gale, Cengage Learning*

Detroit • New York • San Francisco • New Haven, Conn • Waterville, Maine • London

Christine Nasso, *Publisher*
Elizabeth Des Chenes, *Managing Editor*

© 2009 Greenhaven Press, a part of Gale, Cengage Learning.

Gale and Greenhaven Press are registered trademarks used herein under license.

*For more information, contact:*
Greenhaven Press
27500 Drake Rd.
Farmington Hills, MI 48331-3535
Or you can visit our Internet site at gale.cengage.com

For product information and technology assistance, contact us at

Gale Customer Support, 1-800-877-4253
For permission to use material from this text or product, submit all requests online at
www.cengage.com/permissions

Further permissions questions can be e-mailed to permissionrequest@cengage.com

Articles in Greenhaven Press anthologies are often edited for length to meet page require-ments. In addition, original titles of these works are changed to clearly present the main thesis and to explicitly indicate the author's opinion. Every effort is made to ensure that Greenhaven Press accurately reflects the original intent of the authors. Every effort has been made to trace the owners of copyrighted material.

Cover image © Todd Davidson/Illustration Works/Corbis.

**LIBRARY OF CONGRESS CATALOGING-IN-PUBLICATION DATA**

The rising cost of college / Ronald D. Lankford, Jr., book editor.
    p. cm. -- (At issue)
  Includes bibliographical references and index.
  ISBN-13: 978-0-7377-4444-6 (hardcover)
  ISBN-13: 978-0-7377-4445-3 (pbk.)
  1. College costs--United States. I. Lankford, Ronald D., 1962-
  LB2342.R57 2009
  378.3'80973--dc22

                                                                2009009747

Printed in the United States of America
1 2 3 4 5 6 7 13 12 11 10 09

# Contents

# Introduction

Americans often have seen education as the great social equalizer. Regardless of one's class or family background, education has been viewed as a key to social advancement and a ticket to a middle-class lifestyle. In the modern era (after World War II), earning a college degree has become a central component of American education. Furthermore, a general belief seems to have formed around college accessibility: Anyone who wishes to attend college—whether that be a graduating high school student or an individual who has decided to return to school later in life—should be able to do so. While everyone might not be able to attend Yale or Harvard, they could at least attend a state-funded institution or even a community college.

During the last two decades, however, social critics have begun to question these assumptions. Most of their questions revolve around one issue: the rising cost of college. If the cost of higher education continues to rise, will fewer qualified students be able to attend college? If the cost of higher education continues to rise, will college debt outweigh the potential income of a white-collar job? These questions become more troubling when they touch upon the American belief in equality through education. If higher education has ceased to work as a social equalizer because of rising costs, will the stability and expansion of the American middle class itself be threatened?

While these questions are difficult to answer definitively, they do provide a framework for understanding exactly what is at stake with the rising cost of college.

## Can Anyone Attend College?

The question of who can afford college is complex. If necessary, for instance, most students can borrow the money needed to attend college. This option, however, fails to address whether financial aid has kept pace with rising college costs and whether parents have been able to continue their roles as primary contributors to a child's college education. In 2007, *Bank Rate* reported that nearly half of the families who planned to send children to college felt that they could not afford to pay for a child's tuition. Still, nearly three-fourths of these families were willing to make the sacrifice. As a result, however, many of the adults in these families will shortchange retirement funds.

While many Americans will still able to attend college, then, the burden of earning a higher education degree has become heavier. "Higher prices are hitting everyone hard, regardless of income level," wrote Cheryl Allebrand in *Bank Rate*. Other sacrifices made by parents include taking a second job, postponing retirement, and taking out personal loans or second mortgages. Many critics have also argued that federal and state governments have failed to support students by increasing financial aid to appropriate levels.

## How Much Debt Is Reasonable?

Debt is also a complex issue. On the surface, many social critics argue that the average debt for a college graduate—approximately $20,000 in 2008—is not excessive. In fact, this amount—the same cost as a moderately priced car—can be paid back over an extended period of time, causing little financial burden. At a loan rate of 6.8 percent over ten years, this would equal a monthly payment of approximately $230. How reasonable the payment seems, however, is likely to be measured against the average starting salary for a graduate. That average in 2008 was $30,000 a year, a figure that led some critics to ask whether higher education really paid off.

It is also important to understand that the $20,000 figure is an average. In other words, some students graduate with no debt, while others graduate with considerably more. Graduate students, in 2008, averaged $45,000 in debt. In an article on college debt, Liz Pulliam Weston of MSN Money noted the severity of the problem. "I get e-mails from readers who are $30,000, $40,000, or more in debt from student loans and who can't find work in their fields." The combined problem of debt and starting salary also extends beyond the difficulty of making a loan payment. In Weston's article, she notes that many students will put off other long-term goals like planning for retirement or buying a house. "The debts delay people from starting families and building a nest egg toward buying condos," noted Bryce McKibben of the Washington Student Lobby.

Following this logic, people who already have families and mortgages may be dissuaded from returning to college and adding to that debt.

## Quality of Education

One issue that often goes unmentioned related to the rising cost of college and the increase in student debt is the quality of education. Social critics often note that a student who wishes to save money can attend community college for two years; it also has been noted that the cost of attending most state institutions is more reasonable than private schools. Educators note, however, that large public institutions with large class sizes are not necessarily the right choice for all students. Furthermore, a student interested in entering a specific field may determine that her best education opportunities are at more expensive institutions. With higher costs and debt, however, some students may make less desirable choices, potentially affecting the quality of their education.

## Rising Cost and Social Equality

The issues related to the rising cost of higher education are obviously troubling for many students as well as those who wish to return to college. But these issues expand beyond students and potential students, affecting American society at large. In the long term, the rising cost of college challenges many cherished beliefs about education as a social equalizer. Education has been an important component—some would say the central component—in the American Dream of equality, promising everyone who will put forth the effort the opportunity of a better future.

Whether the rising cost of college will impact the growth and stability of the American middle class is debatable. The issue, however, continues to command attention from educators, social critics, and politicians. While few people agree on the proper solutions, most agree that college costs will remain a pressing issue in the near future, and that addressing the rising cost of college is essential to reaffirming and sustaining the American way of life.

# 1

# Why Is College Tuition Rising?

*Liz Pulliam Weston*

*Liz Pulliam Weston writes a finance column for* MSN Money.

*In recent years, many commentators have complained that the cost of college has continued to rise. With the help of financial aid, however, the real cost of college has only risen a small percentage at public and private colleges. Still, a number of factors seem to guarantee that college costs will continue to rise. Colleges are spending a great deal of money to remain competitive in national rankings, spending that includes new dining halls and better faculty pay. The real financial crunch, however, has been created by dwindling financial aid packages and a bigger pool of college applicants. Despite these higher costs, college graduates earn 60 percent more than high school graduates, making the inflated cost of higher education a relative bargain.*

The price tag for a college education rose again last year [2003]. Tuition and fees increased 14.1% for public four-year institutions and 6% for private schools, according to the College Board. The retail cost of a college degree has more than doubled in the past two decades, far outstripping the regular rate of inflation.

Parents facing whopping tuition bills have a right to wonder: Why is this happening, and is there any relief in sight?

The answer to the second question is, unfortunately, no. In fact, tuition increases will probably get worse before they get better. That's because colleges face few reasons to curb prices and lots of reasons to raise them.

Liz Pulliam Weston, "The Real Reasons College Costs So Much," *MSN Money*, 2004. Reproduced by permission of the author.

Before you panic and give up hope of college-educated offspring, though, we should put these price increases in perspective.

## The Real Cost of College

Most students don't pay the retail price for college; they pay a discounted rate, thanks to financial aid packages, which have kept pace pretty well with tuition increases. When grants and other non-loan student aid are factored in, the net cost of college—what students and their parents actually paid to be educated—rose less than 5% for most students between the 1992–93 academic year and 1999–2000, according to the National Center for Education Statistics. The exception: students attending selective private colleges, who paid net costs that were 6.7% higher at the end of the 1990s than at the beginning.

---

*Half to two-thirds of the typical college's budget goes to paying instructional salaries.*

---

## College Is Still a Pretty Good Deal

Despite two decades of rising prices, 68% of full-time undergraduates attending four-year colleges still pay less than $8,000 in annual tuition and fees. The payoff: post-college incomes that are 60% higher than those of high school graduates and that, on average, mean $1 million more in lifetime income.

Those reassuring words don't help much, though, if you're a parent trying to save for a college education that is projected to cost more than your house, or a student facing 40% fee increases in a single year—which is the case at some public universities. (Cash-strapped states are cutting back sharply on their appropriations to public schools, which is leading to massive tuition increases.)

How did we get here? Here are three reasons commonly given for college inflation—along with two more that really explain what's going on:

*Capital spending*: Cornell economist Ronald G. Ehrenberg, in his book *Tuition Rising*, describes a kind of arms race among the nation's top schools to have the best of everything: the best facilities, the best faculty and strong sports teams to engender loyalty among alumni donors.

But it's not just the Ivy League schools that are spending like mad. Colleges that want good rankings with *U.S. News and World Report's* annual college rankings and other college-rating programs shell out big bucks on ubiquitous high-speed Internet access, bigger and better dining facilities, new gyms and concert halls, apartments instead of dorms for students.

A lot of this spending is fueled by endowment funds, which in the go-go 1990s were swelled by a rising stock market and increased contributions from stock-rich donors. Critics make a good argument that at least some of the largesse should have been used to put a lid on prices.

But schools couldn't have justified this spending if there weren't other factors at work.

---

*Blaming higher college costs on the teachers alone really doesn't wash.*

---

*Faculty*: Half to two-thirds of the typical college's budget goes to paying instructional salaries. So rising paychecks are indeed a factor in higher college costs. But few college profs are getting rich.

The median salary for a full-time college educator is $46,300, according to the Bureau of Labor Statistics. The picture is brighter for those who have tenure: Full professors make an average $76,200, according to the American Association of University Professors.

The tenure system and the lack of mandatory retirement can make it tough to oust high-earning but less productive employees.

On the other hand, colleges are holding costs down by using a lot of non-tenured teachers: graduate students, instructors and lecturers. In fact, only 55% to 60% of the typical college's staff is tenured or tenure-track.

So blaming higher college costs on the teachers alone really doesn't wash.

*Productivity*: One factor that keeps inflation muted in the private sector is worker productivity. Technology, equipment and experience tend to help the average worker make widgets faster over time. That growing productivity allows a business to create more products for the same cost.

But colleges aren't in the business of making widgets. Those that try to force greater productivity out of their professors—by increasing class sizes or class loads—often find their strategies backfire. The best instructors leave for better environments, and the colleges' reputations suffer among students and the ranking services that gauge university quality.

There's actually pressure for colleges to be *less* productive, Ehrenberg points out: to shrink class sizes and reduce class loads so professors can spend more time doing research.

The problem with this explanation for rising costs is that it's *always* been true. For the past century, worker productivity in most other fields has soared, while its remained about the same at colleges and universities. That doesn't really explain the most recent bout of inflation.

---

*Until higher prices result in a decrease in demand, there's nothing to put a brake on the tuition hikes.*

---

*Financial aid*: Now we're talking about real stuff. As I noted, most people don't pay the sticker price for college. Scholarships, grants and loans reduce the out-of-pocket cost for the majority of students. (Loans just put off the pain, of course, but few students really think about how much the borrowing is going to cost them in the long run.)

As we've seen with the health-care system, if people aren't feeling the real cost of their purchases, they have less incentive to change their behavior. If you're paying the full tab and Elite University jacks up its rates 10%, you might opt for Just Fine State. If enough others followed your lead, Elite might rethink its pricing.

As it stands, however, Elite just needs to boost your financial aid package by 8% or so, and you'll grumble but stay put.

---

*The number of college-age people is expected to grow from 17.5 million in 1997 to 21.2 million by 2010.*

---

The government has chipped in, as well. Tax incentives like the Hope Credit and the Lifetime Learning Credit, student loan interest deductions and tax-advantaged savings plans like Coverdells and 529 college savings plans have made it easier for many parents to pay for college.

That's not to say we should have less financial aid or get rid of tax incentives—far from it. The system we've got ensures that nearly everyone has access to higher education. But until higher prices result in a decrease in demand, there's nothing to put a brake on tuition hikes.

## Bigger Pool of Qualified Applicants

This is the big kahuna and perhaps the strongest force affecting college prices: demographics.

For two decades ending in 1997, the number of college-age people actually declined. The percentage of this shrinking group that actually attended college, however, shot up: from 47% of high school graduates in 1973 to 65% in 1996. That meant the number of people attending college in the 1990s remained pretty stable.

Now the under-25 set is again on the rise. The number of college-age people is expected to grow from 17.5 million in 1997 to 21.2 million by 2010. The percentage actually attending college is bound to increase further, as fewer and fewer decent jobs remain for those with just a high school education.

Meanwhile, the most selective schools haven't expanded that much, even as the number of qualified applicants keeps rising. That's why the SAT scores that would have gotten you into Harvard a decade ago might not get you accepted at your safety school today.

Many other schools have shelved expansion plans—either because they are state schools with shrinking legislative appropriations or because their endowment funds and giving programs took a hit along with the economy. An economic rebound could reverse that trend, but right now the good colleges have far more applicants than they've got room.

With that kind of demand, college and universities can continue to boost prices almost at will.

# 2

# College Is Still Worth the Expense

*Justin Draeger*

*Justin Draeger writes and lectures on higher education, politics, management, and new media.*

*With the cost of college rising, many have asked a central question: Is a college education worth the cost? The answer, when looking at information gathered from a number of surveys, is definitely yes. The central factor that makes college—even at inflated prices—worth it is the ability of graduates to enter higher work "zones," as defined by the U.S. government. The lower work zones pay the least and are filled primarily by non–college graduates. The highest zones provide the highest incomes and are filled primarily by college graduates. As long as a student is able to borrow minimal funds ($20,000), college easily remains a worthwhile value.*

With average undergraduate debt levels hovering around $20,000 for a 4-year degree, many have asked if going to college is still worth the years of inevitable student loan debt. The answer, according to new report from the Education Research Center (ERC) is a resounding YES!

The report, "Diplomas Count: Ready for What? Preparing for College, Careers, and Life After High School" uses information from the Occupational Information Network, or O\*NET, a database developed for the U.S. Department of La-

Justin Draeger, "Yes, It's Still Worth It," National Association of Student Financial Aid Administrators, June 2007. Reproduced by permission.

bor, and the American Community Survey, conducted by the U.S. Census Bureau, to show the strong, positive correlation between earning power and education level.

With politicians throwing around phrases like "student loan mortgage" and "mortgaging our future" in order to paint a doomsday-like picture of current student debt levels, it is important that prospective students aren't scared off from college by the thought of student loan debt.

As a student borrower myself, I would love to be able to finish my graduate degree without any student loan debt. As it happens, I won't, but I'm not complaining! My personal experiences confirm the findings of the ERC report: more education is worth moderate debt levels.

---

*Higher education levels are especially critical for low-income students who may need to turn to loans in order to meet unmet need.*

---

## Landing in the Right Job Zone

The Occupational Information Network was developed for the U.S. Department of Labor to classify U.S. jobs into one of five categories, or zones. Jobs are placed into each zone depending on worker attributes such as education level, training, and experience needed for that job. According to the ERC, the discrepancies between zones that require high skill and education levels (zone 5 jobs) and those requiring lower education levels (zone 1 jobs) are dramatic. But even more telling are the discrepancies between jobs that require moderate educational training, i.e., some college, and jobs that require no college.

In job zone 3, where almost 40 percent of jobholders have some college education, the median annual income is a little over $35,000. Compare that to the bottom-end of the zone classifications in job zone 1 where the majority of jobholders have a high school diploma or less and the median annual income is less than $13,000 a year, and it is easy to see that even some college is better than none.

Still, the majority of college graduates are likely to end up in job zones 4 or 5, where the median incomes are around $50,000 and $60,000, respectively. Considering that the average student loan debt is less than the price of most new cars, $20,000 seems to be a reasonable price for an education that may yield $50,000 to $60,000 in annual income, and continue to grow for years into the future.

## Labor Market Mismatches

Higher education levels are especially critical for low-income students who may need to turn to loans in order to meet unmet need. The majority of low-income, minority students tend to live in urban areas where zone 5 jobs are available, according to the report. For example, in Washington, D.C., more than 15 percent of all jobs are at zone 5 level, meaning that they require a high level of education, experience, and skills. More than 75 percent of zone 5 job holders in D.C. have at least a bachelor's degree.

But the report notes that ironically, those zone 5 jobs are almost entirely inaccessible to D.C.'s public school students, where 40 percent fail to earn even a high school diploma let alone go on to college. This mismatch between the demand for highly skilled and educated workers and the oversupply of low-income, underserved populations in urban areas is not unique to Washington.

*Students need to understand that college is still worth the price of moderate levels of student loan debt.*

Getting the message out that college is vital to the future economic well-being of these students—in spite of some possible college loan debt—should be part of college access initiatives. The report examines state policies in three key areas:

- College and Work Readiness: Eleven states define what students should know and be able to do to be prepared for credit-bearing courses in college, and 14 states are working on a definition. Twenty-one states have a definition of work readiness, and 10 are working on one. Approaches to defining readiness fall into four major categories: standards, skills, coursework, and assessments.

- Advanced Diplomas: Twenty-four states award advanced diplomas or some type of formal recognition to students who exceed standard high school graduation requirements. But while all of those states award honors for accomplishments in core academic subjects, only eight also provide recognition for accomplishments in a career or technical program.

- Exit Exams: Twenty-two states require exit exams for the class of 2007 and three states—Maryland, Oklahoma, and Washington—plan to do so for future graduating classes. The number of states basing exit exams on standards at the 10th grade level or higher has increased from six in 2002 to 18 in 2007.

Surely there is work to be done to ensure that college access initiatives help prepare students for the real opportunity of college. But in the financial aid community, as part of our message that students should graduate with as little debt as possible, it is important to ensure that students do not forgo postsecondary education entirely for fear of future debt burden. Students need to understand that college is still worth the price of moderate levels of student loan debt. No debt is better than some debt, and while debt-free graduates are a laudable goal, statistically speaking, a future of economic stability is certainly worth $20,000 in student loan debt.

# 3

# College May Not Be Worth the Expense

## Nan Mooney

*Nan Mooney is the author of* I Can't Believe She Did That: Why Women Betray Other Women at Work *and* My Racing Heart: The Passionate World of Thoroughbreds and the Track.

*Because of the rising costs, many have begun to question the value of a college education. Upon graduation, graduates are often burdened with large debts that require a sizable income to repay. Unfortunately, the higher paying jobs are not always available. Simply put, there are fewer good jobs than there are college graduates, and as a result, many graduates work at lower level jobs to get by. The lack of opportunities has led a number of graduates to grow more cynical and question whether college was worth the expense. Only by entering the corporate world can graduates hope to regain the financial investment of college.*

Jayne never expected money to be an issue, not given her master's degree in chemistry from one of the top math and sciences universities in the country. Fresh out of graduate school, she accepted a seemingly secure corporate job working in the lab at a pharmaceutical company. She got laid off after only a year. When she couldn't find another pharmaceutical position, she wound up moving back in with her parents and getting a job at Pottery Barn for $7 an hour, joining a wave of graduates whose diplomas hadn't opened the door to much of anything. In 2004 there were more unemployed college graduates than high school dropouts.

Nan Mooney, *(Not) Keeping Up with Our Parents: The Decline of the Professional Middle Class*. Boston, MA: Beacon Press, 2008, pp. 51–54. Copyright © 2008 by Nan Mooney. All rights reserved. Reproduced by permission of Beacon Press, Boston.

In search of an alternate career, Jayne eventually started substitute teaching in the local school district for $60 a day. She found she loved the interactive dynamics of the classroom far more than the isolated monotony of corporate lab work. Despite her master's degree, it took her two years to find a full-time teaching job in the New Hampshire public school system. Today, at thirty-two, she earns $37,000 year as a high school science teacher, an amount she supplements by teaching organic chemistry one night a week at the local college and working in her father's office during the summers.

"This is my overeducated life," she explains over a patchy cell phone connection while driving from school to school one Thursday evening. "I always have at least two jobs and I still live paycheck to paycheck."

---

*A rise in college-educated workers doesn't ensure more widespread financial security.*

---

## Paying Off Debt

Such lean living made it impossible to pay off the $30,000 in student loan and credit card debt she had accumulated during graduate school. Even her father, a financial planner, couldn't come up with a budget that allowed her meager paychecks to stretch that far. So, while in the process of launching her teaching career, Jayne turned to a debt-consolidation agency for help. Today, she's managed to pay back nearly half the money she owes. She's also going to school part-time to earn her third degree, a master's in education, so she can make a few extra thousand dollars a year as a teacher.

"Even if I eventually get my PhD, the salary cap for high school teachers is around $70,000," she explains. "And that would be many years, and a lot more debt, down the road. Sometimes it's hard to stay motivated when you're earning so little money. And very easy to just burn out."

Jayne's grateful her job feels secure, in that there will always be a need for high school science teachers. But in her current school system the teachers have been working without a contract for the past year, a fact that makes her nervous enough that she's considering moving to another—hopefully higher-paying—district in another state.

"Worrying about money keeps me up at night," she admits. "This was not how I envisioned my future. I was raised to expect that a job and an education would lead to a certain quality of life. That definitely isn't happening here."

## An Oversupply of Qualified Applicants

Simple mathematics assures us that Jayne's experience is far from unique. There isn't a skilled job for every skilled college graduate, and the economy can't be expected to shift to make room for more degree-holders just because they exist. A rise in college-educated workers doesn't ensure more widespread financial security. Instead, it means many wind up in jobs that are below their qualifications, and earn corresponding salaries. Today 37 percent of flight attendants, 21 percent of embalmers, and 13 percent of security guards and casino dealers have college diplomas.

*At one time, taking financial risks was considered part of the middle-class coming-of-age process.*

The oversupply of qualified applicants means employers have little incentive to make those jobs that do require college degrees pay off. Sure, a few budding bankers and corporate lawyers will take a flying leap into six-figure starting salaries, but the average income for a new college graduate is a far more humbling $36,000. Long-term unemployment is also rising for college graduates, increasing nearly three percentage points from 2000 to 2005.

Sabina, a thirty-year-old teacher who grew so fed up with the U.S. academic system that she took her master's in education overseas to work in Vietnam, describes the moment she truly began to appreciate the limits to the amount of security her stellar education could actually provide.

"One afternoon, five of us were sitting in our living room in Baltimore. We were all in our late twenties and early thirties. We had eleven degrees between us. And our total income was less than $100,000. That just made me sick."

## Regretting College

Among the people I interviewed, those freshest out of school seemed the most optimistic about the future, even saddled with debt and low-paying careers. They, most strongly, believed that financial tangles would somehow work themselves out. But over time, those college-instilled expectations created far more conflicted feelings. I found many people in their thirties and older questioning the value of a college education. People who told me that, given the high cost and uncertain payoff, they regretted getting graduate or even undergraduate degrees. Many had stories of friends and family members who'd skipped college—and the accompanying debt—and were making higher salaries as machinists, welders, court reporters, and even baking bagels. They mentioned encouraging their own children to get a profession or a trade, that college wouldn't be a necessity for them.

---

*Today's graduates never get to know the meaning of the words "fancy free."*

---

"Sadly, I would love to get back to counseling," said Caitlin, thirty-two, who works as a product manager for an aviation company to pay off the $60,000 in government and private loans she took out to finance her master's in social work. "But I could never make enough money to pay off my loans or save up for a house. When I started school, I didn't get the ramifications of having so much debt because I'd never had any before. I certainly didn't understand how much money I'd have to make to pay it off."

At one time, taking financial risks was considered part of the middle-class coming-of-age process. These days, those in their twenties who decide to take a year off to write a novel, to accumulate several thousand dollars in debt backpacking through West Africa, to spend six months in cooking school, or even to waste money they don't have buying vintage comic books or CDs or maxing out their Victoria's Secret credit card can pay a tremendous price. I spoke to people who did all these things and, instead of chalking them up to experience, they're working two or three jobs, agonizing over whether they can afford a house or children, and dodging calls from collections agencies, all in an effort to make up for what they lost.

## Postcollege Blues

"I want to go back to school in the worst way," said Amelia, thirty, who left college two semesters short of a biology degree to try to make it as a dancer in New York. Nine years and two ankle surgeries later, she feels closed out of future possibilities. "I want to be a doctor. I applied and was accepted to go back and finish my undergraduate degree, but there's no way I can afford it. I'm still trying to pay off loans from the first time around. Some days I feel optimistic and I think maybe next year. Other days I think I've screwed it up for life."

The postcollege years used to be a time when people had the freedom to test careers, travel the world, screw up a few times before finding their niche. Now, far too often, they exit the ivy-covered walls and make a beeline for the corporate ladder already saddled with enough debt to sink anyone without the luck of, or foggiest interest in, landing a job on Wall Street. Today's graduates never get to know the meaning of the words "fancy free." Instead they're launched into an economic system, a political system, and a value system that teaches its most promising members that the only definition of success is a high-earning job, and that loads them up with enough debt that many young people truly wonder whether there's any other wise choice than the corporate one.

# 4

# Rising College Costs Saddle Students with Postcollege Debt

*Marcy Gordon*

*Marcy Gordon is a reporter for the Associated Press.*

*As college costs have risen, students have been forced to borrow larger sums to support their education. As a result, many former students are now saddled with large debts. With an average debt of $19,000, many University of Washington graduates have found it difficult to buy a house and start a family, a trend that has been seen across the country. This nationwide trend has been supported by the banking industry; in 2006, the industry lent $17 billion and held $85 billion in outstanding student loans. Unfortunately for many borrowers, aggressive marketing and unclear disclosure rates have helped add to long-term student debt. Aggressive lending, however, also has another potential drawback. Critics have argued that because banks have been willing to loan money despite an applicant's qualifications, an economic downturn could lead to widespread defaults.*

The near doubling of the cost of a college degree over the past decade has produced an explosion in high-priced student loans that could haunt the U.S. economy for years.

While scholarship, grant money and government-backed student loans—whose interest rates are capped—have taken up some of the slack, many families and individual students have turned to private loans, which carry fees and interest rates that are often variable and up to 20 percent.

Marcy Gordon, "U.S. College Students Buried Under Debt: Costly Loans Grow, Burden Future Workers," *Seattle Post-Intelligencer*, October 1, 2007. Reproduced by permission.

Many in the next generation of workers will be so debt-burdened that they will have to delay home purchases, limit vacations, even eat out less to pay loans off on time.

Kristin Cole, 30, who graduated from Michigan State University's law school and lives in Grand Rapids, Mich., owes $150,000 in private and government-backed student loans. Her monthly payment of $660, which consumes a quarter of her take-home pay, is scheduled to jump to $800 in a year or so, confronting her with stark financial choices.

"I could never buy a house. I can't travel. I can't do anything," she said. "I feel like a prisoner."

A legal aid worker, Cole said she might need to get a job at a law firm, "doing something that I'm not real dedicated to, just for the sake of being able to live."

---

*Nationwide, more than $17 billion in private student loans were issued last year [2006], up from $4 billion in 2001.*

---

## Borrowing College Tuition

Parents are still the primary source of funds for many students, but the dynamics were radically altered in recent years as tuition costs soared and sources of readily available and more costly private financing made higher education seemingly available to anyone willing to sign a loan application.

Students with no credit history and no relatives to co-sign loans (or co-signing parents with tarnished credit) were willing to bet that high-priced loans were a trade-off for a shot at the American dream. But high-paying jobs are proving elusive for many graduates.

"This is literally a new form of indenture ... something that every American parent should be scared of," said Barmak Nassirian, associate executive director of the American Association of Collegiate Registrars and Admissions Officers.

Holly Johnson, 21, a senior enrolled in the University of Washington's Comparative History of Ideas program, considers herself lucky because scholarships have kept her student debt lower than most.

Still, she worries about how it will affect her life. Seattle's skyrocketing housing prices already make the idea of buying a home seem out of reach. Add to that paying off her loans "and buying a house even after 30 (years old), much less before 30, seems impossible to me."

Johnson also worries about having to take a job "that's not necessarily desirable; that doesn't enrich your life in a non-material way. To put it in layperson's terms, it makes it more likely you'll have to bend over for the man a little bit."

Bryce McKibben, 21, a UW political science junior and president of the Washington Student Lobby, also is fortunate, having received a full scholarship. But his organization, which lobbies for more higher education funding, said on average students in the state graduate with $19,000 in debt.

"The debts delay people from starting families and building a nest egg toward buying condos," he said.

Amy Peloff, 35, a Ph.D. candidate in women's studies, said many students worry about studying abroad—often an once-in-a-lifetime opportunity—for fear of increasing their debt.

---

*The question is whether everyone who borrowed will be able to repay.*

---

## A Nationwide Trend

Peloff said she was able to buy a townhouse in the Central Area by stretching out her own student loans to lower the payments.

Nationwide, more than $17 billion in private student loans were issued last year [2006], up from $4 billion in 2001. Outstanding student borrowing jumped from $38 billion in 1995 to $85 billion last year, according to experts and lawmakers.

Rocketing tuition fees made borrowing that much more appealing. Consumer prices on average rose less than 29 percent during the past 10 years while tuition, fees, and room and board at four-year public colleges and universities soared 79 percent, to $12,796 a year and 65 percent to $30,367 a year at private institutions, according to the College Board.

Scholarship and grant money have increased, yet for almost 15 years, the maximum available per person in government-guaranteed student loans, which by law can't charge rates above 6.8 percent, has remained at $23,000 total for four years. That's less than half the average four-year tuition, room and board of $51,000 at public colleges and $121,000 at private institutions.

Sallie Mae, formally known as SLM Corp., has been on the winning side of the loan bonanza. Its portfolio of 10 million customers includes $25 billion in private and $128 billion in government-backed education loans. However, private-equity investors who had offered $25 billion to buy the company backed out last week, citing credit market weakness and a new law cutting billions of dollars in subsidies to student lenders.

---

*Critics say what happened in the mortgage market could happen in the student loan market.*

---

Citigroup Inc., Bank of America Corp., JPMorgan Chase & Co., Wells Fargo & Co., Wachovia Corp. and Regions Financial Corp. are also big players in the private student loan business. And there has been an explosion in specialized student loan lenders, such as EduCap, Nelnet Inc., NextStudent Inc., Student Loan Corp., College Loan Corp., CIT Group Inc. and Education Finance Partners Inc.

The question is whether everyone who borrowed will be able to repay. Experts don't track default rates on private student loans, but many predict sharp increases in years to come.

## Banks and Lending Practices

Dr. Paul-Henry Zottola, a 35-year-old periodontist in Rocky Hill, Conn., faces paying $1,600 a month on his student loan on top of a $2,300 mortgage payment and $1,500 on the loan he took out to start his practice.

His credit record remains solid, but he owes more than $300,000 in student loans as he and his wife, Heather, an elementary school administrator, raise two young children.

"It would be very easy to feel crushed by it," Zottola said in an interview. "All my income for the next 10 years is spoken for."

Meanwhile, complaints about marketing of private loans—like ads promising to approve loans worth $50,000 in just minutes—are on the rise. The complaints have made their way to lawmakers, who see a need to regulate the highly profitable and diverse group of companies and the loans they make to college students.

In August [2007], the Senate Banking Committee approved a bill that would mandate clearer disclosure of rates and terms on private student loans. The bill also would require a 30-day comparison-shopping period after loan approval, during which time the offer terms could not be altered.

New York Attorney General Andrew Cuomo said many graduates who borrowed owe as much, if not more, than most homeowners owe on mortgages. Unlike mortgages with clear consumer disclosure requirements—even from non-bank lenders—private lending is "the Wild West of the student loan industry," he said in a telephone interview.

## The Student Loan Market

Critics say what happened in the mortgage market could happen in the student loan market. Cuomo, who conducted a nationwide investigation, said the parallels between the two markets are "provocative."

Demand for bundled student loans sold to institutional investors worldwide fueled lending to students. The market for private student loan-backed securities leapt 76 percent last year, to $16.6 billion, from $9.4 billion in 2005, according to Moody's Investors Service.

The student loan-backed securities market has yet to suffer noticeable effects of a global credit squeeze that was triggered this summer [2007] by a mortgage meltdown of borrowers with risky credit.

"Once the economy starts to slow, you're going to see a large increase of these people in bankruptcy court," said Robert Manning, a professor at Rochester Institute of Technology who has written about college students and credit cards.

A 2005 change to bankruptcy law puts private student loans on par with child support and alimony payments: Lenders can garnish wages if someone doesn't pay.

Cuomo's investigation revealed what he calls an "appalling pattern of favoritism" for student lenders that provided kickbacks, revenue-sharing plans and trips to college administrators in exchange for recommended lender status.

## Corruption and Student Loans

Other critics allege widespread corrupt arrangements propelled a student loan boom.

Lenders deny such charges, arguing that industry growth resulted from surging education costs and that higher interest rates are justified for unsecured loans to borrowers with blemished or insufficient credit records.

"Lenders take 100 percent of the repayment risk on flexible private-education loans made to people with limited credit histories, on which they will not get repaid for several years," Barry Goulding, a Sallie Mae official, told Congress last spring.

New regulations could dry up access to education financing, he and other industry executives argue.

Some experts are skeptical, predicting waves of student loan delinquencies and defaults on what is outstanding.

"Should private student loans suffer the same sort of failure as (subprime) mortgages, as students graduate or drop out and find themselves unable to pay, we will do serious damage not only to the lives of many students but also to the economic and social fabric of our country that depends on college graduates for its strength," said Luke Swarthout at the U.S. Public Interest Research Group.

## By the Numbers

- $19,000: average amount of debt students in the state graduate with, according to the Washington Student Lobby

- $17 billion: amount of private student loans issued in 2006, up 325 percent from 2001

- $85 billion: amount all students owe in outstanding student loan debt

5

# College Debt Can Be Managed with New Social Programs

## Elizabeth Warren, Sandy Baum, and Ganesh Sitaraman

*Elizabeth Warren is a professor of law, Sandy Baum is a professor of economics, and Ganesh Sitaraman is a law student.*

*Most Americans agree that attending college is essential to middle-class status in the United States. Rising college costs, however, are creating multiple problems. A number of qualified individuals simply will not attend college, while others will be saddled with large debts from student loans. To resolve these issues, a program called Service Pays should be adopted. Service Pays would allow anyone affordable loans to attend college and also allow loan forgiveness for anyone who worked in public service after graduation. Students who attended four years of college, for instance, would be able to receive one year of loan forgiveness for every year of work in community, military, or international service. A great deal of the cost of the program would be covered by the organizations that benefit from the service work. The long-term economic and community benefits of the program, however, would far outweigh the costs.*

Americans are a contentious lot. They express an astonishing variety of opinions about politics and religion, sports teams and movies, vitamin supplements and workplace dress codes. Differences on questions of social class, the acceptable level of economic inequality, and the importance of economic mobility are particularly sharp. But on one idea we are united: *97 percent of Americans agree that a college degree is "absolutely necessary" or "helpful" to secure a place in the middle class.* In fact, Americans see a college degree as the single most important determinant of a young person's chances of success, the ticket for admission to the middle class.

But it is becoming harder than ever for families to pay for that ticket. And as students increasingly try to shoulder the burden, many are graduating deep in debt—tempering the good news of higher earning potential with the higher risks associated with debt. Many others, including almost 20 percent of low-income high school graduates with high math test scores, do not manage to enroll in college at all within two years of graduation.

If college is the ticket to the middle class, then a new financing mechanism is essential, one that lets students take responsibility for the cost of their own educations without burdening their families unduly, forcing them to make career choices that push them out of public service, or mortgaging their futures. Our *Service Pays* proposal is designed to give every student who wants to work hard an option to pay for college.

---

*The price of college has grown twice as fast as the price of health care.*

---

## The Rising Cost of College

Tuition and room and board now cost more than $12,000 a year at the average public university. Throw in books and a few other basics, and the bill pushes $16,000. To pay that, the average U.S. family of four not receiving grant aid would have to commit 25 percent of its total pretax income.

A private education is even more expensive, averaging almost $30,000 a year for tuition, fees, and room and board.

Even though grant aid is available to the majority of students, many pay a high price for the opportunity to study in these institutions, often more than $100,000 by graduation. Despite the cost, some students need the choices private colleges often offer in terms of size, admissions standards, fields of study, religious affiliations, or geography. Less expensive state schools may therefore not be an option.

---

*An estimated 20 percent to 30 percent of college students have debt burdens so large that they are difficult to manage.*

---

The numbers keep getting worse. After adjusting for inflation, in-state tuition and fees at the average state university have doubled in 15 years. In fact, the price of college has grown twice as fast as the price of health care.

Grants and scholarships once were reserved for the poorest students, but today almost two-thirds of all full-time undergraduates receive them. Even so, this aid is insufficient to close the growing gap between price and family ability to pay. As charges at the average public four-year college grew by almost $5,000 over the decade from 1994 to 2004, grant aid per student grew by only half that. So students and families have increasingly turned to loans. More than 60 percent of public college graduates and nearly 75 percent of private college graduates have taken on debt to pay for college. The median debt load for public college graduates who borrow is $15,500; for students from private colleges, $19,400. Although federal education loans top $60 billion, they cannot meet demand, and students are taking private loans with less favorable terms—now about 18 percent of total education debt.

An estimated 20 percent to 30 percent of college students have debt burdens so large that they are difficult to manage. Students who choose public service or other low-paying careers, who come from low- and moderate-income families, or whose education does not open the anticipated opportunities often begin their adult lives with debts that completely outstrip their earning potential, creating a financial hole from which they may never escape.

---

*College loan forgiveness would be available to anyone graduating from any two-year or four-year accredited school, public or private.*

---

For years, policymakers have worried about how to make college accessible to the poor. Today the middle class is worried, too. Denise Robinson, a Texas schoolteacher, describes putting her daughter through college: "You don't make enough that you're [rich], but you don't qualify for financial aid. We were probably out at least $100,000."

## Making College Affordable for All

College students can shoulder educational costs if they are assured of opportunities to repay loans. A program that features four years of loans, followed by four years of public service to forgive those loans, would be such an opportunity. It would significantly diminish the burden of education debt and keep open the option of public service and other lower-paying but interesting jobs for grads.

- The federal government would increase the amount students can borrow in the unsubsidized Stafford loan program, offering money for four years of college tuition, fees, and room and board to any student who wants it, on the same terms as current student loans. Under Service Pays, students who work in community service after college would be forgiven one year of college expenses for each year of public service work.

- College loan forgiveness would be available to anyone graduating from any two-year or four-year accredited school, public or private.

- The dollar amounts of the available loans would be pegged to average prices at public four-year colleges and universities. Students would have four years to work off those loans.

- Any student, regardless of family income, could borrow the money, but the debts would have to be repaid by ordinary loan repayment or through community service.

---

*Roughly two-thirds of the bachelor's students and half of the master's students will graduate with debt.*

---

With Service Pays, typical students would begin adult life debt-free at 26 with a college diploma and four years of work experience. Students could buy their own tickets to the middle class.

*Serving the Country.* The community service aspect of Service Pays is as important as access to a diploma. America has critical needs in national preparedness, community infrastructure, and education. Many young people would like to do public service, but the low pay combined with college debts often makes it impossible. Service Pays would open new avenues.

*Service at Home.* Community service workers could be assigned to the states to work in public schools, run after-school tutoring programs, clean up public buildings and parks, rebuild roads and bridges, improve the environment, computerize state administrative systems, assist municipal police and firefighters in administrative functions, and organize communities to reduce crime and develop the local economy. Students who work for nonprofits such as Habitat for Humanity or Teach for America would also be eligible. For each year of community service after college, one year of loans would be forgiven.

*Military Service.* Active-duty service would qualify for loan forgiveness. Each year of active-duty service would offset one year of loans. Eight years of reserve service plus six months of active service would translate to four years of loan forgiveness.

*International Service.* The U.S. Foreign Service, an expanded Peace Corps, and an international aid corps (to address emergencies such as tsunamis) would also qualify for loan forgiveness. Each year of service would result in one year of loan forgiveness.

Service Pays would reduce the impact of Baby Boomer retirements from government and could help strengthen community spirit, promote patriotism and service, and improve perceptions of America abroad.

Service-based debt-forgiveness programs that already exist are limited. At AmeriCorps, for example, loans may be forgiven only up to $4,720 per year. Service Pays can build on past successes by expanding educational benefits and directing more energy toward national challenges.

## The Cost of Service Pays

What are the costs? We begin with one central idea: educating our young people will pay off. The GI Bill helped 2.2 million returning World War II soldiers become engineers, scientists, entrepreneurs, and business leaders, fueling the economy and raising the standard of living. It cost $7 billion (about $240 billion in today's dollars). For every dollar invested, however, about $5 were returned over 35 years in higher productivity and tax revenues.

The country would derive similar returns from Service Pays—the services themselves plus increased tax revenue. The average college graduate pays over $5,000 more each year in total taxes than a high school graduate. It is short-sighted to lose long-term benefits by failing to make higher education financially accessible.

In the current school year, students will receive 1.5 million bachelor's degrees and 680,000 associate degrees. Roughly two-thirds of the bachelor's students and half of the master's students will graduate with debt. If 10 percent participated in the Service Pays program and paid off their entire student debt, the cost of forgiving their loans would be about $3 billion. This cost would be borne by taxpayers as an investment in our future.

Some jobs created for the students would be compensated by the federal government; others would be paid with state or local government funds or by the nonprofit organizations that employ the students. Jobs would be entry level, with corresponding wages and benefits. Some of the federal positions would be in the military, but those costs would not be attributable to the Service Pays program. Funding for the Foreign Service and the Peace Corps would be driven by policy decisions. The possible combinations of opportunities make cost estimates difficult, but a federal investment of $500 million could support 25,000 graduates at $20,000 each.

## Long-Term Benefits

For state and local governments there would be the cost of moving an influx of college graduates into public service jobs. Although some federal support might help create the new jobs, the principal burden should be borne by the organizations—whether states or nonprofits—that benefit from the workers. The states could consider in-kind payment as well, such as housing in unused college dormitory space, surplus housing at closed military bases—or for environmental projects, some on-site housing.

At a time when some state budgets are under sharp fiscal constraints, absorbing new, short-term workers could be difficult. But states recognize the long-term benefits to the local economy of a talented workforce. In effect, Service Pays would ask the states to decide if they wanted to recruit college gradu-

ates to put down roots in state; if some states did not partici-
pate, others might expand their job offerings. A well-educated
workforce is our best hope to grow the economy, remain competitive internationally, and fund government needs for health
care and retirement. We are living through a time of big challenges. And big challenges call for big solutions.

# 6

# The College Cost Act Helps to Make College Affordable

*U.S. House of Representatives Committee on Education and Labor*

*The Committee on Education and Labor of the U.S. House of Representatives oversees education and workforce programs that affect all Americans, from early learning through secondary education, from job training through retirement.*

*In 2008 the College Cost and Access Act became law, bringing about several changes that would provide financial relief for students struggling with rising college costs. First, the College Cost and Access Act would increase Pell Grant scholarships and reduce the interest rates on federal student loans. The program also would provide tuition assistance for students who commit to teaching in high-need schools and partial loan forgiveness for those willing to work in public service professions. With these highlights, the College Cost and Access Act promises to make college more affordable to all Americans.*

Starting July 1 [2008], interest rates on need-based federal student loans will drop, making these loans cheaper for millions of college students, Democratic lawmakers announced on a conference call with reporters today [June 26, 2008]. The lawmakers, U.S. Rep. George Miller (D-CA) and Senator Sherrod Brown (D-OH), who were joined on the call by a higher education expert and a student, also highlighted other new financial aid benefits that are kicking in for students this fall as a result of a new student aid law Congress enacted last fall.

U.S. House of Representatives Committee on Education and Labor, "Starting July 1, Students Could See Significant Savings on Federal College Loans, Say Democratic Lawmakers" [press release], June 26, 2008. Reproduced by permission.

Under the College Cost Reduction and Access Act, which was signed into law last September [2007], interest rates on need-based (subsidized) federal student loans will drop from 6.8 percent to 6.0 percent on July 1st—making these loans more affordable for millions of low- and middle-income students. This is the first step toward halving these interest rates—over the next few years these rates will continue to decrease until they reach 3.4 percent.

---

*The interest rate cut will save the typical student borrower beginning college in 2008 about $2,570 on the life of his or her loan.*

---

## Economic Relief

"With our economy putting enormous financial strains on Americans and tuition prices continuing to soar, these new financial aid benefits could not be coming at a more critical time for college students," said Rep. Miller, the chairman of the House Education and Labor Committee, and the author of the law along with U.S. Senator Edward M. Kennedy. "As families continue to explore their financial aid options for the coming school year, it is crucial to make sure that students are fully aware that significant financial relief, whether in the form of cheaper student loans, increased grant aid, or up-front tuition assistance, is available to help them pay for college this fall."

"Everyone who wants to go to college should be able to do so. The College Cost Reduction Act will help Ohio families—and families across the country—pay for college," said Sen. Brown. "Investing in our nation's students means investing in our nation's future. I applaud the hard work and leadership of Chairmen Kennedy and Miller. This legislation is a victory for college students everywhere."

This interest rate cut will save the typical student borrower beginning college in 2008 about $2,570 over the life of his or her loan. Need-based federal student loans are primarily awarded to low- and middle-income students; according to the Congressional Research Service, 75 percent of need-based federal student loan borrowers have family incomes below $67,000. About 5.5 million students borrow these loans each year to help pay for college.

---

*Altogether, the College Cost Reduction and Access Act will boost college financial aid by $20 billion over the next five years.*

---

In addition, the law also provides the following benefits to students for the 2008–2009 school year:

- *Increases the Pell Grant scholarship* by $490 (raising the maximum award to $4,731 for the 2008–2009 year). This is the first of five annual steps toward boosting the Pell Grant scholarship by a total of $1,090 by 2012. About 5.5 million low-income students receive Pell Grants each year.

- *Provides up-front tuition assistance* to college students who commit to teaching high-need subject areas in high-need public schools after graduation. Undergraduate students will be eligible to receive $4,000 in grants each year, for a maximum of $16,000. Graduate students will also be eligible for $4,000 a year in up-front assistance, for a maximum of $8,000.

- *Provides loan forgiveness to college graduates who enter public service professions* after ten years of public service and federal student loan repayments. Eligible public servants include firefighters, public defenders and prosecutors, first responders, law enforcement officers, early childhood educators, men and women serving in the military, and more.

Altogether, the College Cost Reduction and Access Act will boost college financial aid by $20 billion over the next five years—and at no new cost to U.S. taxpayers.

# 7

# The College Cost Act Does Not Help Students Reduce Tuition

*Fannie*

*Fannie is a lawyer in the nonprofit sector who maintains the blog "Fannie's Room."*

*Although the new College Cost Reduction and Access Act of 2007 promised to resolve the issues surrounding the rising cost of higher education, it never addresses the roots of the cause. First, the reduction of interest rates does nothing to reduce the overall cost of college, and the reduction only applies to federal loans. Next, while the size of Pell Grants will increase, they will only do so over a five-year period; even then, they will cover only a small portion of the cost of college. Finally, debtors will have to make payments on their loans for ten years while working in public service to qualify for loan forgiveness. This means that loan forgiveness would benefit only those with large debts. Overall, the College Cost Reduction and Access Act of 2007 fails to address class inequality and the rising cost of college.*

Back when I still believed the government was serious about addressing the rising cost of higher education and in-equalities with regard to access, I received an email update regarding the College Cost Reduction and Access Act of 2007. "Finally," I thought, "a law that might help people attend college!"

Fannie, "My Take on the College Cost Reduction and Access Act of 2007," *Fannie's Room* [blog], April 30, 2008. http://fanniesroom.blogspot.com. Reproduced by permission.

I read through the law, I read the summaries, and I read updates from nonprofits whose very job is supposedly to protect and advocate student/debtor interests. About the law, I saw buzz phrases and soundbites like how the law was going to "strengthen the middle class by making college more affordable" and "encourage and reward public service."

Okay.

The only question I have after all this is why is this law being so highly touted? It comes nowhere near to addressing the roots of our current "cost of higher education" crisis.

---

*In what universe does "not making college more affordable" suddenly mean "making college more affordable"?*

---

That's why I'm going to go beyond the catchy soundbites and examine the claims versus the reality of the House Committee on Education and Labor.

1. *"Strengthen the Middle Class by Making College More Affordable"*

One of the boldest and most appealing political claims about the College Cost Reduction Act is that it purports to make college more affordable.

How does the law "make college more affordable"? By cutting interest rates on loans that you have to take out to pay unaffordable college costs and tuition.

In other words, the cost of college will remain unaffordable, tuition will continue to rise, and 18-year-olds who don't have the luxury of thousands of dollars on hand to pay tuition will "get to" continue paying for college with student loans. It's just that now these students will pay less interest for doing so—that is, they will have to buy less money to borrow money for college from now on.

This lower interest rate applies only to federal loans.

In what universe does "not making college more affordable" suddenly mean "making college more affordable"?

2. *"Increase the Purchasing Power of the Pell Grant Scholarship"*

For those who aren't familiar, the Pell Grant is a small need-based grant that low-income college students can get. First off, the purchasing power of the Pell Grant is relatively small. In 2006, the maximum Pell Grant that the poorest of the poor students received to pay for one year of college was $4,050. The College Cost Reduction Act will increase this maximum amount to $5,400, *over the course of the next five years.*

---

*Pell Grants don't really offer much incentive for poor kids to feel as though any university door is open to them.*

---

Okay, let's be realistic here. The $4,000–5,000 is free money, and that's good. But at the same time the average cost of attending a public university is $12,796 and a private university is $30,367.

From my own experience, I received a Pell Grant all four years of college and, despite receiving a large academic scholarship, I still left undergraduate with a relatively hefty debt load. Of course, in my stubborn insistence for my low socioeconomic status growing up not to be a barrier to attending an "elite" university, I made what I now recognize to be a financially unwise decision to attend an overpriced private school. That experience of being a poor student surrounded by relatively wealthy elites who have the privilege of bragging about various European (insert foreign country) adventures and taking for granted that their parents can and will pay for their college is, I suppose, a whole other blog topic.

My point here is that Pell Grants don't really offer much incentive for poor kids to feel as though any university door is open to them, even if they are qualified to attend that college. In addition, as the Department of Education notes, only students with family incomes below $45,000 are eligible for a Pell

Grant, with most grants going to those with family incomes below $20,000. And, students coming from families with a combined "lavish" income of $45,000/year would be eligible for the lowest Pell Grant amount of about $400/year.

In sum, the purchasing power of the Pell Grant is low and will continue to be pretty low even after this increase. Secondly, many students whose parents *are far from wealthy are not eligible for* Pell Grants and must finance their educations with some combination of scholarships, student loans, and credit cards. Rather than addressing the root causes of always-rising college costs and the higher education "business," a society of two unequal classes is maintained: a class whose parents can and do write tuition checks versus a large class who must finagle some other way to pay for college.

3. *"Encourage and Reward Public Service"*

This one, too, hits pretty close to home for me as I have been working in the public sector for many years. The College Cost Reduction Act allows for someone's remaining federal student loans to be forgiven after 10 years in qualifying public service work.

Exploring this benefit a little more deeply, we find that this provision has many limitations.

In order to qualify for debt forgiveness one has to have made 120 student loan payments on or after October 2007. Fair enough. But basically, you have to work in relatively low-paying public sector while paying down your loans for 10 years. Those who graduate with high debt burdens will clearly benefit over those who graduate with lower debt burdens—as those with lower debt can perhaps pay off their debt within 10 years. So, to be more accurate, this provision really only rewards and encourages those with high debt and low incomes to work in public service.

In addition, your loans must be what are called federal "Direct Loans" held by the Department of Education. Private loans, which have higher interest rates than federal loans, are not eligible for forgiveness. And, federal loans that you have consolidated or that you will consolidate with non-"Direct Loan" consolidation companies are not eligible for forgiveness. I, for instance, consolidated my loans after graduating from law school and so I am not eligible for public service loan forgiveness at all. And, annoyingly, under current regulations, I am not allowed to "unconsolidate" my loans into the Direct Loan program. I suspect that many are in the same boat. (Update: Supposedly, during a one year window starting in July 2008 those in my boat will be allowed to re-consolidate their loans into the Direct Loan system. Let's see if that happens and how many hoops one has to jump through to do so.)

---

*Perhaps I'm a cynical soul but I think this bill is extremely overrated.*

---

In addition, this provision does nothing to reward those who have *already been working in public service*. For people who, for instance, have been working at a nonprofit while paying down their loans for say the past 8 years, their years of public service for purposes of this loan forgiveness provision will still begin in 2007, just as a new graduate's will. Then after 120 payments beginning in 2007, any student loan debt that is remaining will be forgiven.

Fun times.

On the plus side, the list of qualifying public service jobs appears pretty broad and perhaps covers anyone working at a nonprofit organization. But those details haven't been challenged or significantly addressed yet.

## Little Financial Help for the Middle Classes

So, that's my summary of the College Cost Reduction and Access Act of 2007. There are additional provisions I would have liked to discuss, but in the interest of not boring you I limited myself to the above three. My goal here was to provide a different view on the bill as it has been, I believe, wrongly portrayed as a huge benefit to the lower and middle classes. As the Law Career Blog humorously notes:

> "It has been hailed by the House of Representative's Education and Labor Committee as 'the single largest investment in higher education since the GI Bill.' Interestingly, a separate press release from that committee explains that this 'investment' actually comes 'at no new cost to taxpayers.' A cynical soul might point out that this is not so much an 'investment' as is it a 'cost reallocation'...."

Yes. Perhaps I'm a cynical soul but I think this bill is extremely overrated. It fails to address class inequalities with respect to higher education while simultaneously ignoring the powerful and unaccountable student loan industry. Ironically, that the law is greatly hailed by the media, colleges, and politicians appeases lower- and middle-class families who cannot afford college even though the law really doesn't do much for these families.

# 8

# Rising College Costs Should Not Be Subsidized by Government

*Jacob Sullum*

*Jacob Sullum is a senior editor at* Reason *magazine.*

*Subsidizing college loans is a bad idea. College graduates will earn a million dollars more over a lifetime than nongraduates, making the investment in higher education worthwhile. Government subsidies will only add to the inflation: a number of studies have shown a relationship between government aid and tuition increases. One solution for rising college cost would be human capital contracts, a contract system that would allow students to finance higher education against future earnings.*

The Democrats' eagerness to cut interest rates on student loans reflects a time-honored Washington maxim: If it's good, it should be subsidized. In this case, as in most others, the truth is just the opposite: If it's good, there's no need to subsidize it.

According to U.S. Census data, the average college graduate earns about $1 million more over his lifetime than the average high school graduate. That's a pretty good payoff for the investment in tuition, whether the money is borrowed at the rate promised by the Democrats (3.4 percent), at the current government-subsidized rate (6.8 percent), or even at the market rate (now ranging between 7 percent and 11 percent).

Advocates of increased aid worry that the average college student carries a debt of almost $18,000 when he graduates. But owing the cost of a Hyundai Sonata for a loan that yields an extra $20,000 or so in earnings every year does not seem like a bad deal. It's certainly a better investment than the Hyundai.

---

*When someone else is paying part of the tab, consumers do not worry as much about the cost, so the cost tends to be higher.*

---

## Aid Increases Tuition Inflation

Aid supporters also note that the cost of attending college has been rising faster than the rate of inflation for the last two decades. Yet easy money at taxpayers' expense fuels this escalation. Basic economic theory tells us that boosting the demand for a product or service, which is what government loans and grants effectively do, tends to raise its price.

In a 2005 Cato Institute paper, Hillsdale College political scientist Gary Wolfram reviewed the relevant studies and concluded "there is a good deal of evidence suggesting that federal financial assistance has the unintended consequence of increasing tuition for all students." One study found public and private four-year colleges increased net tuition (taking internal aid into account) by 68 cents and 60 cents, respectively, for each additional dollar in Pell Grants. Another study found private colleges raised net tuition by 72 cents for each additional dollar of federal loan aid.

Different types of schools respond differently to increases in subsidies, and price hikes can take several forms, including cuts in state funding and internal aid as well as increases in the official tuition. But the general effect is pretty clear: When someone else is paying part of the tab, consumers do not worry as much about the cost, so the cost tends to be higher.

This phenomenon creates a vicious circle in which subsidies push up prices, leading to demands for increased subsidies, which push up prices again.

Although subsidizing college degrees no doubt has produced more of them, this effect has not been as dramatic as is commonly assumed. "The large majority of the rise in higher education participation in America occurred *before* there was a major federal financial involvement," economist Richard Vedder noted in a December speech at the Heritage Foundation.

## Human Capital Contracts

To the extent that rising subsidies since the 1970s have encouraged people to enter college who otherwise would not have, that is not necessarily a good thing. Citing low completion rates, Vedder argues that "we probably have over-invested in higher education," attracting marginal students who never graduate.

Which makes sense, since anyone who can finish college and reap the typically large returns from doing so should be able to finance tuition through market-rate loans, private aid, or some combination of the two. The nonfederal market, which already accounts for a rising share of student loans, could be augmented by human capital contracts, under which students agree to pay a percentage of their future earnings in exchange for tuition money.

First suggested by the economist Milton Friedman half a century ago, such contracts reduce risks for lenders, especially when combined and sold as shares in an investment fund. They help borrowers with no collateral tap the added income they expect to earn with a college degree.

Given these alternatives, government aid is necessary only when the investment in college tuition is not economically viable. It makes sense only when it doesn't.

# 9

# Faculty Salaries Affect Higher College Costs

*John O. Edwards*

*John O. Edwards is a writer for NewsMax.*

*While many parents and students are struggling to pay for college, professors' salaries have continued to grow beyond the rate of inflation. Teacher salaries, in fact, have been one of the primary reasons for rising college tuition. The high salaries also show that tenured professors have become a special caste, a position that affords them special privileges. Incomes are driven even higher when universities scramble for professors who have published important books in order to boost the colleges' ratings. Compounding the problem are administration salaries, which also continue to rise. Finally, student loans have contributed to rising college costs. Because students can borrow as much as they wish, there is no incentive for universities to keep costs down.*

These are very fat days indeed for America's college professors, who are living high on the hog.

While middle-class parents struggle to pay Junior's way through college, college professors have seen their salaries leap well beyond the rate of inflation—an average increase in 2006–07 of 3.8 percent, outdistancing inflation's 2.5 percent jump.

All this, while the cost of a college education soared by an average of 6 percent in 2006, according to the College Board, straining the load on parents' bank accounts and often leaving new graduates with a massive college loan debt to repay.

---

*At Rockefeller University, the top-paying university in the Unites States, full professors pull down an average salary of $186,400.*

---

"On average, 75 percent of the costs to run a college are related to personnel expenses, including benefits," states a position paper for the Secretary of Education's Commission on the Future of Higher Education. "Faculty salaries are especially expensive, particularly in high-demand subject matter areas like business and engineering."

David Horowitz, author of "The Professors" and publisher of *FrontPage Magazine*, a leading critic of higher education, tells *NewsMax*, "What is driving the cost of higher education is the higher cost of salaries—combined with government guarantees of student loans."

## The Professor Caste

"The professor caste is the most privileged caste in America today," Horowitz says. "Once they have tenure, they have lifetime jobs with four months paid vacation every year and sabbaticals. In return, they may teach only six or seven hours a week, or two classes a semester. They can be completely incompetent, but you can't fire them. Salaries can be 80 percent of the cost of running an institution ... If they had to teach 12 hours instead of six, it would dramatically reduce the tuition charges, because you would need half as many people."

Education writer Naomi Rockler-Gladen says, "Being a professor pays much better than it used to, and professors in the sciences get paid pretty well." "Pretty" well? At Rockefeller University, the top-paying university in the United States, full professors pull down an average salary of $186,400. Harvard pays an average of $177,400; Stanford $164,300; Princeton $163,700; the University of Chicago $162,500; and Yale $157,600.

But even in academia, there are haves and have-nots. If you earned your doctorate in medieval Lithuanian poetry, you're not likely to retire young.

---

*Colleges . . . are scrambling to hire more, and better, professors.*

---

The American Association of University Professors (AAUP) annual survey found that professors in the areas of business administration and management are paid the most, followed by professors of communications, computer and information sciences, economics, education, and engineering. Only then do professors of fine arts get to line up at the trough.

Strikingly, the AAUP also found that in the hallowed halls of academia, where feminism and "equal pay for equal work" are virtually worshipped, female professors still make less than male professors. The AAUP noted that on average, male professors in four-year institutions annually earn $10,000 more than female professors.

## "Star" Professors

AAUP's John W. Curtis, director of research and public policy, worries that professors atop the salary food chain might be "more concerned about their own careers than the profession."

The scramble for a college education, resulting in a higher-paying career, is driving students into colleges and universities in greater numbers than ever before.

The National Center for Education Statistics estimates there were 17.3 million students enrolled in degree-granting institutions in 2005, but expects that number to leap to 18.8 million by 2010 and nearly 19.5 million by 2014.

Colleges, therefore, are scrambling to hire more, and better, professors. This creates a supply-and-demand situation that strongly favors the professors, who have their hands out for the biggest salaries.

---

*Colleges are battling back—in a way—by hiring more adjunct and part-time instructors.*

---

"Celebrity culture has invaded the campuses," Mark Bauerlein, professor of English at Emory University and director of research and analysis at the National Endowment for the Arts, tells *NewsMax*.

"Professors become 'stars' by publishing popular books or appearing in the media. The pursuit of these stars became the way for universities to boost their rankings. This created a money chase after celebrities.

"It has become a prestige economy, which causes salaries to increase astronomically. Some of these celebrity professors have played the markets unconscionably."

Arthur Kraft, dean of the business school at Chapman University, says that high salaries in business disciplines result from competition between academia and the business world for hiring top-flight business instructors. He tells *Inside Higher Education* that new accounting and finance professors demand, and receive, 20 percent to 25 percent more than professors in economics or human resources.

## Administration Salaries

But professors aren't the only culprits in the academic goodie grab. A music professor at a private four-year college, who asked not to be named says, "The biggest sponges are the administrators—the people deans answer to. They make tons of money."

In fact, some college administrators pull down $1 million salaries, with a recent College and University Professional Association for Human Resources survey of presidents of four-year public and private colleges discovering that many of them enjoy pay and compensation packages of at least $500,000.

Audrey Williams June writes in *Chronicle of Higher Education*, "The median salary of college administrators increased by 4 percent in the 2006–07 academic year."

The previous year, the jump was 3.5 percent. June notes that it was a "pace that exceeded the rate of inflation for the 10th consecutive year."

"Both faculty and administrative salaries are problems," Bauerlein says. "There are few labor groups in human history who complain more about working conditions and salaries than professors. But in truth, if professors had to work somewhere else, they would appreciate their situations a lot more than they do."

## Hiring Part-Time Instructors

Colleges are battling back—in a way—by hiring more adjunct and part-time instructors, turning over more classroom instruction to graduate students and, generally, shifting work to people who do not rate the high salaries of tenured instructors.

"When you go from tenured to adjunct or part-time instructors, it is a giant leap downward in salary and compensation," Bauerlein says. "Many of them don't have medical or retention benefits and are paid by the course. They have no professional stature or long-term security."

Oddly, this may be a better educational deal for students. "The top-level people often spend a lot of their energy avoiding contact with students," Bauerlein says. "They have a research agenda, a conference paper to deliver, or a book they've been working on for five years. They are often distracted and lazy, whereas adjunct people throw themselves into teaching and bring more commitment to students."

However, the AAUP and the American Federation of Teachers (AFT) have expressed concern about the gap between tenured and part-time and adjunct professor compensation. The AFT is planning a push to require 75 percent of university classes to be taught by full-time professors, and bringing adjunct and part-time professor pay and benefits to "parity" with full-time professors.

Among 160,000 professionals in higher education represented by the AFT, about 60,000 are adjunct or part-time instructors—and the numbers are growing.

If the AFT initiative succeeds, even in part, the result is bound to be a further increase in the cost of college salaries— and a concurrent increase in the cost of higher education.

## Government Money

"The real thing driving the high cost of education is government guarantees of student loans," Horowitz tells *NewsMax*. "The universities have no limit on cost. They can raise their prices and run up their costs at will, because they government has put a floor under it all. It's a bigger scandal than Enron!"

Recent scandals in the student loan industry may well be the first crack in a tottering system, which may cause legislators to take a closer look at the unholy alliance between professor salaries and the high cost of college education.

As the cost of a degree outpaces inflation and even the ability of government grants to help low-income students finance college, more students have turned to private loans and built up huge post-college debts. The average now is $22,000, according to the College Board.

Further, June writes, $1 million salaries being paid to college administrators means that legislators are likely to start "seeking the logic behind high pay for leaders of nonprofit organizations."

# 10

# Faculty Salaries Do Not Affect Higher College Costs

**Doug Lederman**

*Doug Lederman is an editor for* Inside Higher Ed.

*In 2006, the Future of Education Commission issued a paper that focused on the role of faculty salaries in the rising cost of college. The paper complained that universities are forced to compete for teachers, driving salaries higher. Furthermore, it complained that professors, not student demand, control the curriculum, forcing students to attend college for more than four years to complete the required classes for a bachelor's degree. While many within higher education agreed with a number of points made by the commission, they were nonetheless bothered by the strident tone of the paper. Administration salaries, for instance, are rising faster than faculty salaries, and many faculty activities—such as research—are dictated by the institution, not the professors. Overall, the report distorted the role that professors play in the rising cost of tuition.*

Until now, as the Secretary of Education's Commission on the Future of Higher Education [a nineteen-member commission formed by the U.S. secretary of education in 2005 with the goal of reforming postsecondary education] has questioned how well colleges teach their students and blasted the higher education accreditation system, college professors have largely remained off the radar, at least of the panel's public deliberations.

That changed Wednesday [April 2006] as the commission released the latest of its "issue papers" designed to stimulate discussion, including one aimed at identifying "the major factors that induce institutions to spend (and charge) more" and exploring "what's being done—and can be done—about managing college costs and improving affordability."

While the paper proffers many reasons why colleges' costs and, in turn, prices have risen—competition for students, excessive government regulation, subsidies of sports programs—it returns again and again, in ways large and small, to lay the problem at the feet of the faculty.

---

*Faculty leaders were predictably miffed at the report's emphasis on the faculty's role in the college cost problem.*

---

## Hidden Costs

A section on the "hidden costs" that drive up prices, for instance, contains six items, four of which are tied directly or indirectly to the work of professors. A portion on the labor-intensiveness of colleges notes that "faculty salaries are especially expensive," as colleges "compete with each other ... for 'top' faculty." Another part of the paper on why it takes students longer to complete a four-year degree says that the courses that students need are often unavailable—because colleges "do not schedule courses on a student-demand basis, retaining instead a faculty-driven scheduling system."

Elsewhere the paper, which like last week's on accreditation was written by Robert C. Dickeson, is much more directly critical of faculty behavior. Tenure, it says, has changed from a way to protect academic freedom to a "system to protect job security," which hurts institutions by impairing their ability to adapt their curriculums to changing student demands and making it harder for them to get rid of ineffective "dead wood." "The decision to tenure has an accompanying long-term price tag that easily exceeds $1 million per person," the report says.

Most strikingly, the report paints a picture of professors as king makers, dictating campus policies that turn the institutions into bastions of inefficiency. "To understand the management of a college one must understand the unique culture and extraordinary power of the faculty. To many faculty, they *are* the university." Dickeson writes. This power gives professors authority over all curricular decisions and overinvolves them in other campus policy making, resulting in a "slow-moving pace of change;" puts too much power in the hands of department chairs "neither trained in nor committed to management;" and emphasizes "research over instruction as the key to the internal reward systems," among other problems.

---

*These kinds of pithy generalizations are dangerous, given the bias in the public against tenure.*

---

## A Misinformed Report

Faculty leaders were predictably miffed at the report's emphasis on the faculty's role in the college cost problem. Roger Bowen, general secretary of the American Association of University Professors, called Dickeson "woefully misinformed," pointing out that recent salaries have shown administrators' salaries to be growing at significantly quicker rates than those of professors, which have trailed inflation in recent years.

But even experts who've advocated greater productivity by colleges—and by extension, professors—questioned the tone of the paper's comments about the faculty, even while accepting as fact some of its underlying statements.

"These kinds of pithy generalizations are dangerous, given the bias in the public against tenure," said Carol A. Twigg, president of the National Center for Academic Transformation. She called "a little troubling" a section in which Dickeson decries as "abuse" policies that give professors relief from teaching to do research or do other institutional duties, which the paper says have reduced teaching loads to "12, or nine, or six, or, in some cases, three or even zero credit-hour responsibilities."

"Faculty are being released, presumably, because they're doing other things that the institution deems to be important, not to go on vacation," Twigg said, adding that the paper also appears to exaggerate the faculty's power by "assuming the administration has no role in all of these decisions."

## Achieving Their Purpose

The papers released Wednesday, like their predecessors, are designed, the commission said in an accompanying e-mail, "to inform and energize the public about key postsecondary issues and inspire continued national dialogue around the future of higher education in America."

That they are certainly doing. With the commission scheduled to hold its next meeting beginning today [April 6, 2006] in Indianapolis . . . many people who are watching the panel's discussions unfold with intense interest suspect that these papers are a set of trial balloons designed to help the commission's chairman, Charles Miller, and its members decide where support is strongest and opposition is fiercest to the various vague concepts, controversial ideas and solid proposals it is kicking around.

In some cases, as with last week's paper that called for replacing the regional accreditation system with a "national accreditation foundation"—the panel is putting out reasonably well-formed plans. In others, it favors general concepts, as in the case of the other paper the panel released Wednesday, on the federal financial aid system. That paper, prepared by Barry D. Burgdorf and Kent Kostka, vice chancellor/general counsel and a lawyer, respectively, at the University of Texas System (where Miller was chairman of the Board of Regents), argues that the nearly two dozen federal student aid programs "create undue complexity and confusion among users," "countervailing incentives and disincentives for buyers of higher education," and are "overlapping and, in some cases, redundant."

It calls for "harmonizing" and consolidating the programs, asking: "In sum, why not have one federal grant program, one federal loan program and one uniform tax benefit schedule, or better yet one program with complimentary facets all working together in concert to achieve common, well-articulated goals?" Yet it stops short of directly recommending that, most likely because that would unleash howls of protest from advocates for the government's many other grant and loan programs.

---

*Blaming faculty for more and more focus on research doesn't make sense—those are mandates that come down from boards to presidents to change the institution.*

---

The paper on college costs, by contrast, holds little back. It acknowledges ways in which external forces have driven up colleges' own costs, including the explosion of utility and health care costs and the expansion of federal, state and local regulation, and it cites steps that "some institutions" are taking to bring down their costs:

- hiring more part-time instructors or offering multiple-year contracts instead of tenure

- outsourcing of "non-mission-critical functions"

- reallocating resources from "lower to higher priorities"

- offering dual enrollment programs with secondary schools

## A Flawed Report

But much more of the paper is dedicated to colleges' flawed and inefficient practices. The institutions "maintain large physical infrastructures"—libraries, power plants, theaters, stadiums—that are "rarely used to capacity." They "add new programs ... without corresponding cuts in existing" ones. They charge the same for high-cost and low-cost programs. They make "administrative errors in personnel cases" that result in "hundreds of examples annually of judicial awards and countless other out-of-court settlements."

Besides the concern about how "release time" for professors has driven down their teaching loads, the section on "hidden costs" describes redundancies in course offerings and overly long lists of majors, and criticizes academic departments for inflating the number of credit hours required for a major, "thus 'justifying' the number of faculty positions required to be sustained."

Some institutions earn praise. "Why do community colleges cost so much less than traditional four-year colleges?" the paper asks and then answers: far fewer tenured professors, little or no research, instruction-focused physical infrastructure. And two-year institutions "typically prioritize their programs more readily, and are more likely to operate on a business model: conducting market research to determine consumer demand, and dropping programs that don't prove to be efficient or effective."

For-profit institutions come in for similar kudos, for similar reasons: "The curriculum is fixed, the outcomes are measurable, and teachers are held responsible for results," the paper says. "There is a fundamental shift in organizational expectations to 'What's it going to take to satisfy students?' from the traditional, 'What's it going to take to satisfy faculty?'"

Donald E. Heller, associate professor and senior research associate at Pennsylvania State University's Center for the

Study of Higher Education, echoed Twigg's view that the paper seemed to blame faculty members alone for policies and directions that were largely dictated by trustees and presidents.

"Blaming faculty for more and more focus on research doesn't make sense—those are mandates that come down from boards to presidents to change the institution," said Heller. "You're also talking about a very small slice of higher education here, the top tier of institutions, where faculty have a very, very strong role in governance and colleges engage in bidding wars for star professors."

"Cost increases and price increases have been universal across higher education, and at the vast majority of institutions," he said, "faculty are not powerful at all."

# 11

# Tuition Reforms Will Make Ivy League Schools Less Affordable

*Peter Sacks*

*Peter Sacks is the author of* Tearing Down the Gates: Confronting the Class Divide in American Education.

*While Harvard's decision to lower costs for middle-class students may seem like altruism, America's most prestigious university had another motive. Despite Harvard's reputation, there are a number of equally good schools that cost a great deal less to attend. This left Harvard competing for a limited pool of the most desirable students, the sons and daughters of upper-middle-class professionals. Increasingly, colleges have been willing to offer merit aid to attract these students, a practice that has helped push the cost of tuition higher. With Harvard's new policy, a family with an income of $180,000 could save $18,000 a year on tuition. This policy may be good news for the families of these students, but it does very little for the truly needy. Worse still, Harvard's policy will most likely trigger similar policies at other elite universities.*

Harvard's decision to drastically reduce tuition costs for "middle" income families has some observers gushing with praise for America's richest and most powerful university.

But it's not completely out of altruism that Harvard has slashed costs to families earning as much as $180,000 a year—a

Peter Sacks, "Harvard's Middle-Class Makeover," *Tearing Down the Gates* [blog], December 27, 2007. http://tearingdownthegates.blogspot.com/2007/12/harvards-middle-class-makeover.html. © 2007 Peter Sacks. Reproduced by permission of the author.

"middle" income only in the rarefied world of elite college admissions. America's richest and most powerful university has cut costs for such families in order to preserve its dominance as America's richest and most powerful university.

## Competing for Students

Despite its market power, Harvard's Achilles' heel is the practical wisdom of certain upper-middle-class American families. These families have a number of good college choices for their high-achieving children, particularly some flagship public universities that offer an equivalent or better education at a fraction of Harvard's cost.

All colleges want these certain students, the sons and daughters of affluent professionals who attend excellent schools, live in safe and attractive neighborhoods and—most important—score well on their SATs. They also boast extracurriculars that Mother Teresa would envy. It's a good thing because, in this rarefied world, even such high-flying students have to "walk on water" in the lingo of admissions professionals, to have any chance of being admitted to places like Harvard.

---

*As a policy maker you'd be happy with the transfer of wealth from the needy to upper middle class because they vote more often than poor people.*

---

Colleges covet such students, not because the SAT is the final word on one's potential for college success. In fact, colleges know that the SAT is the proverbial emperor with no clothes. Rather, they love such students because they add prestige to the institution. That's because institutional prestige is largely a function of its selectivity, measured by median SAT scores, and that selectivity is a dominant factor in the *U.S. News & World Report* rankings game.

Colleges want these students so much that they're willing to pay for them—bribe them, really, in order to entice them to enroll. Under the guise of "merit," colleges in recent years have drastically increased the amount of scholarship money they offer high-scoring students.

## Merit-Aid Arms Race

What's wrong with that? Nothing if your objective is to take limited scholarship funds from the truly needy students who wouldn't be able to afford college without financial aid. And nothing's wrong with that if you're a policy maker who isn't concerned about raising the overall college-going rates in your state. That's because the "merit" scholarships go most often to relatively affluent students who would be going to college regardless of the scholarship money. Still, as a policy maker you'd be happy with the transfer of wealth from the needy to upper middle class because they vote more often than poor people.

*We know that more college degrees mean better jobs and a more productive citizenry.*

Many top public universities have been among the most aggressive in playing the merit aid arms race, and that's an irritation for the pricey privates like Harvard. . . . Harvard's brand name just isn't worth it for [the] price-conscious families of high-flying students who, in effect, get paid to attend the less costly public institutions.

By limiting the attendance costs to no more than 10 percent of family income, Harvard's move will produce a windfall of savings to the select few upper-middle class families whose children are admitted. A family earning $180,000 would see its Harvard bill drop from about $30,000 to $18,000.

Depending on whether you consider a family earning $180,000 a year as "needy," then it's a matter of debate whether that windfall represents "need" based or "merit" based aid. If you believe that such a family ought to rethink the new Volvo or reconsider the kitchen remodel in order to pay for a Harvard education, then Harvard's bold move is but thinly disguised merit scholarship program for the upper middle class. (It's worth noting that, according to the Census Bureau, a family earning $180,000 puts it in the top 5 percent of household incomes nationwide.)

## Bad News for the Financially Needy

All this is great for Harvard. It's great for those few students who now choose Harvard over a public flagship university. Harvard's applicant pool and its admissions selectivity will bust through the roof, as families who previously thought Harvard was out of reach financially will now apply. Harvard's *U.S. News* ranking will surge.

But this is potentially bad news for American higher education. Other universities will respond with their own versions of "middle class" tuition relief. They will jockey for market position, and the merit-aid arms race will escalate.

That's all to the detriment of truly needy students and their families who will see a fall off in need-based financial aid programs, as colleges increasingly target the very students who already have high rates of college attendance.

At stake is the nation's economic future. Policy makers are struggling to find ways to increase college attendance among families in the bottom half of the income distribution. We know that more college degrees mean better jobs and a more productive citizenry. If Harvard wants to help something other than itself, it would find ways to contribute to that project.

# 12

# Tuition Reforms Will Make Ivy League Schools More Affordable

*Anya Kamenetz*

*Anya Kamenetz writes for* Yahoo Finance *and is the author of* Generation Debt.

*In 2007, a key policy change at Harvard helped make an Ivy League education more affordable. Other colleges, including Yale, soon followed Harvard's lead. The media, however, was skeptical, believing that Harvard was only seeking to avert government regulation. Despite this skepticism, Harvard's policy was actually good news for urban high school students: if a student's family earned less than $60,000 a year, she could attend the university free of cost. While Harvard's policy will not solve the problem of rising tuition, it is helping to set the tone for much-needed reform.*

"If Your Family Earns Less Than $60,000 a Year, Harvard University Is Free."

That's what it read, in bold letters, on the poster I saw hanging on a door at New York City's Legacy High School, where I was attending a planning meeting for community members involved in public schools.

Harvard announced this decision last March, and followed up with an even more generous adjustment in December, de-

Anya Kamenetz, "Getting an Ivy League Education—On the Cheap," *Yahoo Finance*, January 30, 2008. Copyright © 2008 Yahoo! Inc. All rights reserved. Reproduced by permission.

claring that families with incomes below $180,000 a year—all but the top 5 percent of U.S. earners—would pay no more than 10 percent of their income in college costs.

Yale followed suit with a similar announcement a couple of weeks ago, and Princeton, the University of Pennsylvania, Swarthmore, Haverford, Dartmouth, Duke, and Bowdoin have all lowered the expected costs for families making up to six figures, in a new acknowledgement that middle-class and even upper-middle-class families can have trouble affording college.

*Whatever the private colleges' true motivation, . . . these new tuition policies are good news for all families and students who are struggling to pay for a college education.*

## The Skeptical Media

Most media coverage of the change has argued that these tuition policies, while good news for a small number of families, are unlikely to sweep the nation. More than 80 percent of American college students attend public colleges that don't have the same resources to cut tuition costs even if they wanted to.

The skeptical view is that these private colleges, with their multibillion-dollar endowments, are simply trying to get out ahead of government regulation.

In the past decade, many private colleges have hired professional investment managers and made risky hedge fund investments, earning an average of 15.2 percent in 2006—all tax-free, of course. Harvard has grown its endowment from $7 billion to $35 billion since 1991 by pursuing this strategy.

Sen. Chuck Grassley (R-Iowa) has been scrutinizing these practices and backing a new law that would require the 76 private colleges with endowments over $1 billion to pay out at least 5 percent of the money a year, a rule that applies to charitable foundations. Small coincidence then that Harvard and Yale's new policies happen to increase their endowment payouts to right around that 5 percent line.

## Price Slashing Good News for All

Whatever the private colleges' true motivation, however, these new tuition policies are good news for all families and students who are struggling to pay for a college education. The reason goes back to that poster at Legacy School.

Harvard carries a disproportionate symbolic weight. An urban public high school like Legacy may send one graduate there every other year, at most, but knowing that an Ivy League education will be free or affordable for middle-class and working-class students who qualify can motivate millions of young people. In contrast to middle-class students with college-educated parents, low-income students, especially the children of immigrants or the first in their families to attend college, are more likely to be unfamiliar with the confusing student aid applications and to be daunted by high sticker prices.

---

*With tuition rising at two or three times the rate of inflation, the college accessibility "crisis" has many causes, and it will take many different types of reform to address it.*

---

Harvard's publicizing their free-tuition policy may help high-achieving students of few resources get the message that a private college may ultimately be able to offer them more assistance than the local public or community college. And more colleges may feel motivated or pressured to show that they care just as much about affordability as the big names do.

Luke Swarthout, a higher education associate at the U.S. Public Interest Research Groups, agrees that the decisions made by certain schools can have a real impact.

## Harvard and Yale Setting the Tone

"Harvard and Yale clearly set the tone," he says. "They drive the market for students and for faculty. There's a real trickle-down effect.

"To the extent that they encourage states and other institutions to focus on addressing real challenges, like access by low-income students, [Ivy League schools] can be a real force for good and progress."

The trickle-down effect has already begun. At a recent meeting of the University of California Board of Regents, a research group headed by UC Berkeley Chancellor Robert Birgeneau cited the Harvard and Yale decisions when recommending that the public university system create a $2 billion fund from private donations and tuition, and dedicate it to reducing college costs.

The University of California system is one of the largest in the world, with over 200,000 students. It also does a better job than many other large state systems at helping community college students transfer in and complete their degrees. A decision in California to redouble the resources dedicated to access would have a positive effect on a large number of students who really need the help.

The study found that within 10 years, even with existing student aid, the cost of attendance for students from families making less than $40,000 a year will average $16,700 or more, an amount that the chancellor called "unrealistic."

## Guaranteeing Accessibility

"Our ultimate goal is to guarantee accessibility for the indefinite future, not only for students from the poorest families but also for those from the middle class," he said in a statement. "It is urgent that we act now to avoid a crisis of accessibility in the near future."

With tuition rising at two or three times the rate of inflation, the college accessibility "crisis" has many causes, and it will take many different types of reform to address it. The cause that's gotten the most attention of late in Congress and on the presidential campaign trail has been the role of the federal government—the largest provider of tuition assistance—and the need to use taxpayer resources more efficiently so we're subsidizing students, not just student loan companies.

The recent decisions by a few private colleges raise the stakes for other educational institutions to show that they're dedicated to holding down costs for students. I believe it's now time for families and communities to push for more accountability and transparency on the part of public institutions. Colleges need to show that they can be efficient in their use of resources and do more with less. Competition and smart consumer choices by students and families will ultimately be just as important to holding down college costs as contributions from the public and private sector combined.

# 13

# Community College Is an Affordable Option

*Richard Vedder*

*Richard Vedder is a distinguished professor of economics at Ohio University and the author of several books, including* The American Economy in Historical Perspective.

*While community college enrollments usually have increased during difficult economic times, the recent growth in attendance at two-year schools also has been part of a long-term trend. Because the cost of four-year institutions continues to rise, many students are choosing to attend more economical community colleges. The rate of return for attending a four-year school has also dwindled: the job market no longer justifies the level of investment for a private college. A number of students are learning that many jobs do not require a four-year education while others have been happy to attend community college for two years and then transfer to a more expensive four-year school. Community colleges may not suit everyone's needs, but they do offer a welcome choice in the face of rising college costs.*

The papers are full of news that community college enrollments are booming, suggesting this is a byproduct of an economic downturn. When times are tough, people go to Wal-Mart instead of Sak's Fifth Avenue, and to community college instead of four-year universities.

The data suggest, however, that the trend to two-year schools is more long-lived. Today's [August 23, 2008] *USA To-*

Richard Vedder, "Rising Community College Enrollments," *Center for College Affordability and Productivity* [blog], August 23, 2008. http://collegeaffordability.blogspot.com/2008/08/rising-community-college-enrollments.html. Reproduced by permission.

*day* features a graph that shows that a majority of the increase in college enrollments since 1995 has occurred at the two-year schools. This is in marked contrast to the picture from, say, 1975 to 1995, when the market share of community colleges was actually declining. Those schools were viewed as inferior, and as an increasingly affluent American population chose schools, they mostly wanted the qualitatively superior four-year option. Community college market share fell for the same reason bus transportation was losing its market share— there were qualitatively better alternatives.

## Rising Community College Enrollments

Why, then, the change since 1995? Two factors are relevant. First, while the cost of college has been rising generally, the increases are particularly profound at the four-year schools, in my judgment because universities typically are deemphasizing undergraduate instruction and using incremental tuition funds to finance lower teaching loads, more administrative hires, more luxurious student facilities, etc. As the cost differential between two- and four-year schools grows, more are selecting the lower cost alternative.

---

*Colleges are screening devices—separating the bright and motivated from the less bright and lazy. They are damnably expensive screening devices.*

---

Second, the dirty little secret in higher education is that the gains from going to college have stopped increasing altogether for women, and have slowed and arguably stopped for men, particularly when one considers the time to get a bachelor's degree today is more often five rather than four years—and many do not graduate at all. In short, the gains from going to college are not growing, and may be even declining, while the costs of college continue to increase. The rate of return on private college investment is falling. More people, faced with the college decision, are compromising, going to two-year schools knowing they have the option of switching to the more expensive four-year alternative for the last two years (one of my Whiz Kids, Bob Villwock, has done precisely that, and very successfully).

When I was on the Spellings Commission [the Commission on the Future of Higher Education known as the Spellings Commission because it was created by U.S. Secretary of Education Margaret Spellings.], I argued that you could dramatically slow the growth in average college costs simply by increasing the proportion of students attending community colleges, finding myself often in agreement with the commission's sole community college member, Charlene Nunley. My support for non-traditional post-high-school training has been enhanced by recent research that Gordy Ruchti has done for Andy Gillen and me for a new book, research that shows that an awful lot of the new jobs being created DO NOT NEED college-level training. Further convincing me is Charles Murray's great new book, *Real Education*, which my friend Ben Wildavsky gave a lukewarm review of in yesterday's *Wall Street Journal* but which I think is brilliant, like such previous Murray books as *Losing Ground* and, with Richard Herrnstein, *The Bell Curve*.

## A Welcome Alternative

Community colleges are not perfect. They have extremely high attrition rates, they often have qualitatively suspect offerings, etc. But on the whole they are very much oriented toward undergraduate instruction, are relatively inexpensive, and lack the elitist superiority attitudes that dominate the four-year selective universities. While I suspect the four-year public schools on balance these days are anti-egalitarian and on net reduce equal economic opportunity in this country, that is clearly not the case with the community colleges.

Colleges are screening devices—separating the bright and motivated from the less bright and lazy. They are damnably expensive screening devices. The two-year schools can help reduce the cost of screening, just as can alternative approaches, such as vocational certification/testing, on the job training programs, etc. Harvard may be number one in *U.S. News's* book, but I equally admire the Montgomery Community Colleges (the school my friend Charlene used to head) of the world—schools that make a difference in more people's lives—at less cost.

# 14

# Rising College Cost Is an Obstacle to Low-Income Students

## Richard D. Kahlenberg

*Richard D. Kahlenberg is a senior fellow at the Century Foundation, where he writes about education, equal opportunity, and civil rights.*

*As college costs have risen, there has been a growing disparity between those who can afford to attend college and those who cannot. This is particularly evident at selective colleges, where children from wealthier families form the majority of the student body. Many have nonetheless argued that the current system is balanced, and that there is room for all qualified students. A number of studies, however, have suggested otherwise. Low-income students may be disadvantaged in elementary and secondary schools, but many have continued to qualify for elite schools. Colleges, however, have focused more on merit scholarships (for which anyone can apply) than traditional student aid. As a result, low-income students are underserved by the college system in the United States.*

In a country where education is supposed to be the premier vehicle for promoting equal opportunity and social mobility, college costs and financial-aid policies still keep too many students from making the transition from high school to college.

To be sure, lack of adequate preparation in elementary and secondary schools, and the competition among colleges for the "best" students, play a role. Something else is at work, however, when, according to Thomas G. Mortenson, roughly one in two students from families making more than $90,000 obtain a bachelor's degree by age 24 compared with one in 17 students from families making less than $35,000 a year.

At selective colleges and universities, disparities are especially stark. At the 146 most selective institutions, according to a 2004 Century Foundation study by Anthony P. Carnevale and Stephen J. Rose, 74 percent of students in 1995 hailed from the richest socioeconomic quartile and just 3 percent from the bottom quartile. Put differently, wandering around one of the nation's selective campuses, you are 25 times as likely to run into a rich student as a poor one.

## Are Rich Students Smarter?

So are rich kids 25 times as likely to be born smart as poor kids? No serious people believe that.

No doubt low-income students are less prepared academically than higher-income students: They are more likely to come from educationally disadvantaged homes, to attend lousy schools, and to have SAT scores that lag 200 points behind those of higher-income students.

According to the congressionally created Advisory Committee on Student Financial Assistance, only 34 percent of low-income eighth graders go on to graduate from high school qualified for college. For some observers, the story ends there. Greg Forster and his co-author, Jay P. Greene, argue in a Manhattan Institute working paper that, by their estimation, there were 1,299,000 college-ready kids in the year 2000, while 1,341,000 actually entered college that year. Another recent Manhattan Institute paper comes to a similar conclusion. Ipso facto, the papers deduce, there is no large pool of college-ready poor kids being denied access to higher education because of financial need.

---

*Put badly, the dumb, rich kids had as much chance of going to college as the smart, poor ones.*

---

That line of reasoning would be news, presumably, to the families sitting around thousands of kitchen tables across the country and concluding that their bright children will have to forgo a four-year public college because they have no idea how to come up with the $3,800 in annual "unmet need." That's the sum of college expenses beyond the expected family contribution and student aid that low-income families face, according to the Advisory Committee on Student Financial Assistance.

The Manhattan Institute's calculations are more stringent in defining who is "college ready" than those used by the National Center for Education Statistics. But let's assume that the institute's estimates are right and that the number of college-ready students is roughly the same as the number of students enrolled. Isn't it possible that the numbers line up so neatly because some dumb rich kids are attending college, while some smart poor and working-class kids are being shut out?

## Smart, Low-Income Students

The research clearly shows that, controlling for ability, low-income students are much less likely to attend college than high-income students. In a study conducted by John B. Lee, 78 percent of students in the lowest economic quartile and highest achievement quartile as measured by standardized tests had enrolled in postsecondary education within two years, compared with 97 percent of high-achieving students of high socioeconomic status—almost a 20 percentage-point difference. Moreover, 77 percent of students from the lowest achievement quartile and highest socioeconomic status attended college in the same time frame.

Put badly, the dumb, rich kids had as much chance of going to college as the smart, poor ones. Another study found that 48 percent of college-qualified low-income students did not attend a four-year college within two years of graduation, compared with 17 percent of high-income college-qualified students.

---

*Researchers have found that even the most elite institutions could substantially increase the number of low-income students without sacrificing quality.*

---

These data raise serious questions about the role of financial need. The inadequacy of financial aid is the result of conscious decisions by policy makers not to keep up with the rising costs of college. The Pell Grant for low- and moderate-income families, for example, used to cover nearly 40 percent of the average total cost of attending a four-year private college, but now covers about 15 percent.

## Financial Aid and "Strivers"

Colleges, too, are to blame, channeling scarce resources, in order to boost their own rankings, toward financial aid for students who have high SAT scores and families that can afford to pay for their education.

According to Kenneth E. Redd, director of the National Association of Student Financial Aid Administrators, need-based grants still make up the bulk of grant aid and have increased 110 percent, from $18.6 billion in 1994 to $39.1 billion in 2004. But merit scholarships, given without regard to need and tending to benefit the better-off, rose at an even faster clip during the same period, from $1.2 billion in 1994 to $7.3 billion in 2004—a 508 percent increase.

Research by the policy consultant Arthur M. Hauptman finds that, at many private institutions, students from high-income families are nearly as likely to receive aid as students from low-income families.

At selective colleges, another barrier also keeps out low-income students: an admissions system that fails to give them a leg up. Virtually all colleges claim to provide an advantage to "strivers"—students who have overcome tremendous odds to perform quite well. A student from a low-income, single-parent family who attended mediocre schools and managed to do well despite those hardships is generally considered more meritorious than a student who had a comparable or even somewhat better academic record but achieved it with private tutors and all sorts of other advantages.

In reality, however, the rhetoric about providing affirmative action for low-income students turns out to be quite hollow. The Century Foundation study found that the most selective 146 institutions showed racial preferences that essentially triple the combined percentage of black and Latino students to 12 percent from the 4 percent that would be admitted under a system considering only grades and test scores. But the share of students enrolled from the bottom economic half is actually slightly lower (almost 10 percent) than would be admitted under a system of admissions strictly by grades and test scores (12 percent). William G. Bowen, outgoing president of the Andrew W. Mellon Foundation, came to a similar conclusion in his study of 19 highly selective colleges and universities.

## Low-Income Students Underserved

Do universities admit few low-income students because they fear that the students will not do well—the "preparation" issue the Manhattan Institute emphasizes? Again according to the Century Foundation researchers, no: There is a rich supply of highly capable low-income students who could do the work at selective universities. The researchers say that at the institutions they studied, a system of "class-based affirmative action"—admission based on grades and test scores with a preference for low-income students—could see the number of students from the bottom economic half rise from the current 10 percent to 38 percent without any decline in graduation rates.

Other researchers have found that even the most elite institutions could substantially increase the number of low-income students without sacrificing quality.

None of this is meant to minimize the enormous issue of preparation. On one level, conservatives are right to argue that K–12 reform is the key to improving college access for disadvantaged groups. But we shouldn't hold our breath for elementary and secondary education to provide genuine equal opportunity anytime soon. The problem with the "fix K–12" approach is that it starts a cascade of blame shifting. Higher education blames K–12; K–12 blames its failures on low-income families and inadequate preschool education. Pretty soon, we're all left focusing on the pregnant mother's womb.

By all means, let's work toward adequate nutrition and education for pregnant mothers, and good preschool and K–12 systems too. But inequality in higher education is more complicated than the issue of preparation alone, and colleges and policy makers have crucial roles to play in providing a leg up to low-income students in admissions and ensuring sufficient financial aid. To say the problem is not at all about money is just as silly as to say it's only about money.

# 15

# All Costs Must Be Considered When Choosing a College

## *Sallie Mae*

*Sallie Mae is the nation's leading provider of student loans and administrator of college savings plans.*

*A study was completed by Gallup and Sallie Mae in the summer of 2008 that suggested that despite rising college prices, cost was often not taken into consideration when choosing a college. Many families also failed to balance borrowed funds against future incomes and the ability to repay loans. Overall, many families are failing to plan ahead for college, leaving them less prepared to meet expenses. Families have chosen to pay for college in a variety of ways including, on occasion, credit cards. Middle-income families currently borrow more to meet college expenses than low- or high-income students.*

College students and their parents see higher education as a critical investment in the future, but according to a national study of college-going families released today [August 20, 2008] by Sallie Mae and Gallup, many overlook the cost of college as they select their school and do not consider post-graduation income as they decide whether and how much to borrow to pay for college.

The study of 1,400 undergraduate students and parents, "How America Pays for College," reveals that:

- While 58 percent of families reported ruling out schools because of cost at some point during the application process, another 42 percent of families did not limit their search based on cost—even after reviewing financial aid packages.

- In total, 70 percent of students and parents said a student's expected post-graduation income either was not considered or did not make a difference on their borrowing decisions.

- Sixty percent of parents are worried that institutions will raise tuition, followed by 51 percent noting concern that loan rates will increase. Significant percentages of parents also expressed anxiety that student loan money will be less available, their savings will decline, or the value of their homes will decrease.

- While credit card use for college expenses is relatively low in total (3 percent of students and 3 percent of parents charged part of their expenses), those who used credit cards to pay for college cited emergency cash flow problems as the No. 1 reason.

- Three percent of all families reported tapping home equity to contribute nearly $11,000 toward their child's college education last year. Nearly three-quarters (73 percent) of these parents plan to borrow against home equity again to fund their child's education for the coming school year.

- While nearly nine out of 10 families (89 percent) with annual income below $35,000 filled out the Free Application for Federal Student Aid (FAFSA), this number drops off considerably to only 76 percent for families with annual incomes between $35,000 and $50,000, and continues to fall as income rises.

## Lack of Financial Planning

"While the study once again illustrates the importance of a college education to Americans, it also points to areas of focus for all of us interested in higher education," said C.E. Andrews, president, Sallie Mae, the nation's leading provider of saving- and paying-for-college programs. "For example, too few parents and students are focusing on the total cost of college, not enough are using available college savings tools, too many are borrowing without considering how they will repay, and too many are not completing federal financial aid forms that enable them to access free federal financial aid and lower-cost student loans. For our part, Sallie Mae is committed to making it easier for families to navigate the financial aid system. For example, we counsel customers to follow a '1-2-3 approach' to paying for college so that they exhaust grants and scholarships, explore federal loans and fill any gap with private education loans."

---

*The study suggests that middle-income families tend to borrow more to afford a higher-cost postsecondary institution.*

---

According to the "How America Pays for College" study, parents, on average, footed the largest portion of the college tuition bill, through current income and savings (32 percent of the total amount paid) and borrowing (16 percent), while the average student covered 33 percent of the cost, through borrowing (23 percent) and their own income and savings (10 percent). Scholarships and grants covered another 15 percent of the higher education price tag, with the remaining 3 percent contributed by relatives and friends. The most often used source was parents' current income, rather than savings, with

38 percent of all families spending an average of $5,815 last school year. Only 9 percent of families used college savings funds, such as a 529 plan, but of those who did, the average amount contributed, $7,964, was the highest source of any personal contribution.

How America pays for college varies across income levels. Higher-income families paid much more from savings and income, and generally paid substantially more for college. Lower-income families received the most "gift aid," such as scholarships and grants, while middle-income families borrowed the most, both in real dollars and as a percentage of their total college costs. The study suggests that middle-income families tend to borrow more to afford a higher-cost postsecondary institution.

Slightly less than half (47 percent) of all families borrowed money to pay for college, and federal student loans were the top source for both students and parents. Additional details on borrowing follow:

- Twenty-eight percent of all students used federal student loans, borrowing an average of $5,075 last school year.

- Federal Parent PLUS Loans were used by 6 percent of all parents, at an average loan amount of $10,701.

- Eight percent of all students and 4 percent of all parents used private education loans, with average amounts of $7,694 and $6,910, respectively.

- One percent of all parents borrowed from their retirement accounts. Another 3 percent of all families took an early withdrawal from their retirement savings to pay for college.

As part of the company's longstanding commitment to financial literacy, Sallie Mae recently launched the Education Investment Planner, a free, comprehensive online tool that enables families to estimate the total cost of a college degree, build a customized plan to pay for college, and estimate the salary a graduate would need to keep repayment of student loans manageable. Sallie Mae's Education Investment Planner helps families understand the total cost of college and how to pay for it without going beyond their means.

# Organizations to Contact

*The editors have compiled the following list of organizations concerned with the issues debated in this book. The descriptions are derived from materials provided by the organizations. All have publications or information available for interested readers. The list was compiled on the date of publication of the present volume; the information provided here may change. Be aware that many organizations take several weeks or longer to respond to inquiries, so allow as much time as possible.*

**American Enterprise Institute (AEI)**
1150 17th Street, NW, Washington, DC   20036
(202) 862-5800 • fax: (202) 862-7177
Web site: www.aei.org

AEI is a conservative public-policy institute that provides research and educational materials on social, political, and economic issues in the United States. The institute promotes policies that advocate limited government, private enterprise, individual liberty, and a vigilant defense and foreign policy. With regard to education, AEI scholars focus their work on assessing all aspects of the American education system and the need for reform with an emphasis on topics such as school financing and parental choice, the No Child Left Behind Act, accountability in education, and teacher education and certification. Articles on these topics and others can be found on the institute's Web site and in AEI's bimonthly magazine, *The American*.

**American Policy Center (APC)**
70 Main Street, Suite 23, Warrenton, VA   20186
(540) 341-8911 • fax: (540) 341-8917
e-mail: ampolicycenter@hotmail.com
Web site: www.americanpolicy.org

APC is a grassroots organization committed to promoting free enterprise and limited government regulation in both commerce and individual life. The center contends that the free market provides the best opportunities for individuals and the United States as a country to realize its full potential. APC argues against increased federal involvement in the U.S. education system because it believes that the federal government's management of public education has not benefited American students. Articles outlining current problems and possible solutions for education in America can be found on the APC Web site as well as in the monthly publication of the organization, *The DeWeese Report*.

### The Brookings Institution
1775 Massachusetts Avenue, NW
Washington, DC   20036-2188
(202) 797-6000 • fax: (202) 797-6004

Founded in 1927, the Brookings Institution is a liberal think tank that conducts research and provides education in government, foreign policy, economics, and the social sciences. The institute publishes the *Brookings Review* quarterly as well as numerous books and research papers.

### Center for a New American Dream
6930 Carroll Avenue, Suite 900, Takoma Park, MD   20912
(301) 891-3683
e-mail: newdream@newdream.org
Web site: www.newdream.org

The Center for a New American Dream is an organization whose goal is to help Americans consume responsibly and thus protect the earth's resources and improve the quality of life. Its Kids and Commercialism campaign provides information on the effects of advertising on children. The center publishes booklets and a quarterly newsletter, *Enough*.

## Center for Character and Citizenship
402 Marillac Hall, One University Boulevard
St. Louis, MO  63121-4499
(314) 516-7521 • fax: (314) 516-7356
e-mail: ccc@umsl.edu
Web site: www.characterandcitizenship.org

The Center for Character and Citizenship is an organization within the University of Missouri–St.Louis's College of Education that provides scholars, educators, and organizations with information about the development of moral and civic character and the tools needed to foster these traits in students. The center publishes the *Journal of Research in Character Education* as well as individual reports such as *What Works in Character Education: A Research-Driven Guide for Educators*. Articles from the journal, copies of center reports, and additional resources all can be accessed on the center's Web site.

## Coalition for College Cost Savings
1031 17th Avenue South, Nashville, TN  37212
(615) 242-6400 x213 • fax: (615) 242-8033
Web site: www.thecoalition.us

The Coalition for College Cost Savings (CCCS) is a group of nonprofit organizations that work together to reduce operating costs at private institutions of higher education. Increased efficiencies will allow member institutions to better serve their students, faculty, and communities.

## The Heritage Foundation
214 Massachusetts Avenue, NE, Washington, DC  20002-4999
(202) 546-4400 • fax: (202) 546-8328
e-mail: info@heritage.org
Web site: www.heritage.org

The Heritage Foundation is a conservative public-policy organization that promotes policies that align with the principles of free enterprise, limited government, individual freedom, traditional American values, and a strong national defense.

The Heritage Foundation believes that good governance on the state, not federal, level and allowing parents to choose the right school for their children are the best methods for improving education in the Untied States. The foundation's Web site provides topical articles on these and other issues.

**Kettering Foundation**
444 North Capitol Street, NW, Suite 434
Washington, DC   20001
(202) 393-4478 • fax: (202) 393-7644
Web site: www.kettering.org

The Kettering Foundation was formed in 1927 as a nonprofit research institution that studies problems of community, governing, politics, and education, with a particular focus on deliberative democracy. It publishes the periodicals *Kettering Review* and *Connections* as well as the National Issues Forum book series.

**The National Center for Public Policy and Higher Education**
1100 New York Avenue, NW, Suite 1090 East
Washington, DC   20005
(202) 292-1020
Web site: www.highereducation.org

The National Center for Public Policy and Higher Education promotes public policies that enhance Americans' opportunities to pursue education and training beyond high school. The center prepares action-oriented analyses of policy issues facing the states and the nation regarding opportunity and achievement in higher education. The center communicates performance results and key findings to the public, civic, business, and higher education leaders along with state and federal leaders.

**National Council on Measurement in Education (NCME)**
2810 Crossroads Drive, Suite 3800, Madison, WI   53718
(608) 443-2487 • fax: (608) 443-2474

Web site: www.ncme.org

NCME works to advance and improve the science of measurement in the education field so that assessment can be more useful for improving education in the United States. NCME publishes the quarterly *Journal of Education Measurement* and the quarterly *Educational Measurement: Issues and Practice*.

**National Education Association (NEA)**
1201 16th Street, NW, Washington, DC   20036-3290
(202) 833-4000 • fax: (202) 822-7974
Web site: www.nea.org

NEA is a professional organization open to employees of public schools, colleges, and universities. On the local level, NEA volunteers and affiliate organizations raise funds for scholarship programs and bargain contracts for school district employees, among other activities. At the state and national levels, NEA affiliates lobby legislators on behalf of their members and public schools in an effort to protect academic freedom, ensure the rights of school employees, and increase the effectiveness of public education. NEA opposes vouchers, supports the use of professional pay to recruit and retain quality teachers, and works to ensure that the achievement gap of low-income and minority students is reduced. *NEA Today* is the organization's monthly magazine.

**Progressive Policy Institute (PPI)**
600 Pennsylvania Avenue, SE, Suite 400
Washington, DC   20003
(202) 547-0001 • fax: (202) 544-5014
Web site: www.ppionline.org

PPI works to define and promote progressive public policy through research, policies, and education. In the area of education, the institute focuses its research on improving teacher quality, increasing school choice, strengthening accountability, and expanding the implementation of innovative strategies in public education. Articles outlining the institute's stances on these educational topics and others can be found on the PPI Web site.

## U.S. Department of Education

400 Maryland Avenue, SW, Washington, DC   20202
(800) 872-5327
Web site: www.ed.gov

The Department of Education was established by Congress on May 4, 1980, with the goal of improving education nationwide through the use of federally mandated education programs. Initiatives have focused on establishing policies on federal financial aid for education and distributing as well as monitoring those funds. The department publishes a variety of newsletters on specific topics relating to education; all of these and other publications and reports can be accessed online.

# Bibliography

## Books

| | |
|---|---|
| Trent Anderson and Seppy Basili | *Paying for College: Lowering the Cost of Higher Education.* New York: Kaplan, 2007. |
| Ronald G. Ehrenberg | *Tuition Rising: Why College Costs So Much.* Cambridge, MA: Harvard, 2002. |
| Richard H. Hersh and John Merrow, eds. | *Declining by Degrees: Higher Education at Risk.* New York: Palgrave Macmillan, 2006. |
| Tim Higgins | *Pay for College Without Sacrificing Your Retirement: A Guide to Your Financial Future.* Richmond, CA: Bay Tree, 2008. |
| Chuck Hughes | *What It Really Takes to Get Into Ivy League and Other Highly Selective Colleges.* New York: McGraw-Hill, 2003. |
| Anthony T. Kronman | *Education's End: Why Our Colleges and Universities Have Given Up on the Meaning of Life.* New Haven, CT: Yale University Press, 2008. |
| Harry Lewis | *Excellence Without a Soul: Does Liberal Education Have a Future?* Jackson, TN: Public Affairs, 2007. |

Nagesh Narendranath · *Beating the College Sticker Shock: A Step-By-Step Plan to Beat College Costs No Matter Where You Start.* Lincoln, NE: iUniverse, 2005.

Peterson's · *Paying for College: Answers to All of Your Questions About Financial Aid, Scholarships, Tuition Payment Plans, and Everything Else You Need to Know.* Lawrenceville, NJ: Author, 2008.

Corey Sandler · *Cut College Costs Now!: Surefire Ways to Save Thousands of Dollars.* Cincinnati, OH: Adams Media, 2006.

Edward P. St. John and Michael D. Parsons, eds. · *Public Funding of Higher Education: Changing Contexts and New Rationales.* Baltimore, MD: Johns Hopkins University Press, 2004.

Richard Vedder · *Going Broke by Degree: Why College Costs Too Much.* Washington, DC: AEI Press, 2004.

Gordon Wadsworth · *Cost Effective College: Creative Ways to Pay for College and Stay Out of Debt.* Chicago, IL: Moody, 2000.

Yale Daily News Staff · *The Insider's Guide to the Colleges, 2009: Students on Campus Tell You What You Really Want to Know.* New York: St. Martin's Griffin, 2008.

Liang Zhang · *Does Quality Pay? Benefits of Attending a High-Cost, Prestigious College.* New York: Rutledge, 2005.

# Periodicals

| Cameron Ainsworth-Vincze | "The Bottom Line," *Maclean's*, November 24, 2008. |
| --- | --- |
| Joy T. Bennett | "Finance 101: Money-Management Skills for College Students and Parents," *Ebony*, September 2008. |
| Arian Campo-Flores | "Harvard Hits the Rich-Poor Gap," *Newsweek International*, August 25, 2008. |
| Jane Bennett Clark | "Uncle Sam Wants (to Thank) You: the New G.I. Bill Offers Military Veterans a Generous Reward," *Kiplinger's Personal Finance*, September 2008. |
| Kim Clark | "49 States Flunk College Affordability Test," *U.S. News and World Report*, December 3, 2008. |
| Kim Clark | "Pass Around the Cap," *U.S. News and World Report*, April 21, 2008. |
| *Community College Week* | "Budget Slumps Force Mass. Colleges to Hike Fees," May 26, 2005. |
| Heather Grennan Gary | "Sticker Shock: Are Catholic Colleges and Universities Worth the Price of Admission?" *U.S. Catholic*, November 2008. |
| Tim Goral | "Open Textbooks Aim to Cut College Costs," *University Business*, September 2008. |

Kimberly
Lankford

"Paying the College Bills," *Kiplinger's Personal Finance*, July 2008.

*Legal Intelligencer*

"Tackling the High Cost of Higher Education," May 27, 2008.

*Long Island Business News*

"Paying for College Is Tough, But Not Impossible," October 31, 2008.

M.H. Miller

"Report: Rising College Costs Outstripping Student Aid," *Community College Week*, August 1, 2005.

Kimberly Pye

"Scholarship Secrets," *Careers and Colleges*, Fall 2008.

Don Rauf

"The Real Cost of College," *Careers and Colleges*, Fall 2008.

Yuval Rosenberg

"House Rich, College Poor," *Money*, April 2008.

Jeff Schlegel

"College Saving Savvy," *Working Mother*, April 2008.

Anne Tergesen

"Scoring a Private Loan for College," *Business Week*, May 12, 2008.

Matthew Tuttle
and Angelo J.
Robles

"Finding Ways to Lighten the Tuition," *Accounting Technology*, April 2008.

Penelope Wang

"Is College Still Worth the Price?" *Money*, September 2008.

Jill Waterman

"Free Tuition?" *Photo District News*, April 1, 2008.

Kevin Williamson    "Debt or Equity? Options for Funding Higher Education," *National Review*, October 20, 2008.

Lauren Young    "College Costs: Coping with the Meltdown," *Business Week Online*, October 8, 2008.

# Index